Making the Invisible Visible

The Human Principles for Sustaining Innovation

Making the Invisible Visible

*The Human Principles for
Sustaining Innovation*

Robert B. Rosenfeld

with

John Kolstoe

Contents

PART I: THE INNOVATION PROCESS: ITS ESSENCE

PART II: THE INNOVATION PROCESS: ITS ENVIRONMENT

ENDORSEMENTS

"Bob Rosenfeld has devoted a lifetime to understanding innovation, and has distilled his knowledge into this clear, compelling and useful guide. His focus is on human dynamics: the passion, pain, processes and values that underlie successful innovation. Through storytelling and a wealth of examples he brings eight principles of innovation to life. Any business facing an imperative to change could benefit from Bob's insights."

—*Don Hall Jr., President and CEO: Hallmark Cards, Inc.*

"An innovation that has a chance of success within an organization often lands there with the impact of a thistledown on a warm summer afternoon. It takes extraordinary skill and human empathy to design innovation approaches that can catch this innovation and develop it into it's full potential. Bob Rosenfeld, as one of the premier innovators of our time, brilliantly lays out the underpinnings of these approaches and gives us wonderful insight into the full rich tapestry and interrelationships of the human component that is the quintessential ingredient in any successful innovation undertaking. This is 'Must' reading for those developing or implementing innovation systems in the business world today."

—*Peter J. Engstrom, Vice President for Corporate Knowledge Creation, Science Applications International Corporation*

"Bob Rosenfeld, a dedicated and passionate ombudsman for ideas and the people who have them, has finally set down in book format his true wealth of knowledge about the innovation process. Bob's insights come from more than 25 years of practicing the craft of innovation within large organizations both as an employee and as a consultant. It is time for many more people to come to know and understand this truth if innovation is successful on a regular basis."

—Stan Gryskiewicz, Ph.D., Senior Fellow: Creativity and Innovation, Center for Creative Leadership

"Making the Invisible Visible is a true practitioner's view of the underlying principles for sustained innovation . . . many of which are a controlled by organizational culture and individual interactions which are the invisible enablers (or impediments) behind (or preventing) breakthrough innovation. This is a graduate course for managers or individuals accountable for sustained growth through innovation within their organizations."

—Gary Wilhelmi, Director: New Business Development, Frito-Lay-PepsiCo

"Making the Invisible Visible brings principles and practices of innovation to life through an approachable and thoughtful process. This is not merely a book, it is truth. I have expereinced Robert Rosenfeld's work in practice. He has a unique ability to blend the realities of business environments with the truths of human nature so that real innovation can happen. His approach works—it supports how innovation can make a positive difference to both people and the bottom line of an organization."

—Lucy Swift, Vice President, Marketing, UnitedHealthcare

ACKNOWLEDGEMENTS

I grew up in a post-war Brooklyn ghetto of the Jewish variety. Apartments then were crowded with humanity—with aunts, uncles, neighbors, and cousins; with food and feasts and the motion of bodies and the energy of ideas. Around the dinner table were discussions that everything seemed to depend upon: the Holocaust, politics, business, art, and Faith. In the clash of different views, new ideas took exhilarating form.

Every life is a collection of images and influences. Today, as I look around that dinner table in my mind's eye, I am struck by how grateful I am to the people who have populated my life. There are those who shaped my mindset, others who came to my assistance at crucial periods. I am happy to have the opportunity to name just a few of them.

In the family of my childhood, business was oddly juxtaposed with art and political awareness and the awareness of humanity. I must thank my father, Leo, who was my first example of a businessman from the old school, and my mother, Sylvia, who supported him throughout his life. My Uncle Sol, who became the head of DC Comics, was a businessman with an intensely creative flair and his wife Gert is, to this day, a deeply humane woman who exemplified service to the weak and frail. I owe them all a great debt in my early formulation of what it meant to participate in the world.

Never thinking that I would myself become a businessman, my first job was as a chemist at Eastman Kodak Company in

Rochester, New York. There, as I eventually set up the "Office of Innovation," I was generously mentored by several people who saw the potential in a young man with a wild beard and sometimes even wilder ideas. In particular, I must thank Bob Bacon, Bob Tuite, Dick Vickers, and Tom Whiteley, each of whom taught me, by excellent example, what the best of innovation leadership could look like. I was also assisted by very skilled, committed, and loyal individuals who made the Office of Innovation happen: Gail Hofferbert, Jim Stephens, and Jack Thatcher.

At a certain point in my career, I found myself in a community of people within the field of creativity studies. Stan Gryskiewicz, Peter Engstrom, and Dorothy Marcic have all been deep and abiding friends who have shared their opinions about ideas and much, much more.

When I finally decided to venture out on my own and create Idea Connection Systems, I began a journey where I've been lucky enough to share my path with gifted, exceptional partners. I am deeply indebted to each of them. Jenny Servo, a psychologist and consultant, crystallized a world of new ideas for me early on—ideas that became essential to my work as a whole. Michael Winger-Bearskin was overwhelmingly creative and fantastic fun with whom to "ping" ideas back and forth. David DeMarco combined a talent for penetrating analysis with an open, innovating mind. Carey Corea, my business partner since 1996, has an incredible ability to boil issues down to their essence.

At Idea Connections, I've also been blessed with excellent guidance. I thank Becky Murphy, Marty Harrison, Larry VanEtten, Richard Agent, Leonard Smith, Barry Rabson, and Robert Henderson for their honest and invaluable council. There have also been those who worked tirelessly at the painstaking details, without whom this company would simply have ceased to function long ago. MaryAnn Hussar, Janet Meier, Kim Wykes, Linda Pickert, Joyce Perry, and Don Braun must all be singled out. In all honesty, I need to thank every one of the many people who have worked for Idea Connections over the years. I've tried to make the company a haven for people who share common values—people with life-paths that are sometimes unusual, but who have all contributed to the rich pageant that is this company.

Michael Winger-Bearskin once said that the clients we work with create everything from "fuzzy bunnies to nuclear weapons." It's marvelously true that Idea Connections' clients come in very different forms. Respecting the privacy of the companies I work with means that I will not name them here. Suffice it to say that each of my clients has taught me invaluable lessons about diversity and innovation. Several of them have become true friends. To all of them, I am profoundly grateful.

Looking at it one way, this book should have been impossible to write. I am dyslexic, something I only understood as an adult when my daughter was diagnosed with the same condition. I've always struggled with reading and writing, but as I watched my daughter grow up, seeing some of myself in her, I realized that although my dyslexia has been a handicap, it has also been a gift. It caused me to read people, rather than the ink on a page. It taught me to read whole situations—with their intellectual, emotional, and political layers—instead of paragraphs. At 57 years old, I am finally grateful for what seemed to be, for so long, an unwieldy cross to bear.

Because of the dyslexia, the writing of this book became yet another many-faced adventure. Several people, all friends, came together during the process of translating onto paper what was in my head. John Kolstoe, a writer and member of my Faith, understood my mental models and value system. Maggie Paxson, an anthropologist, read with a careful critical eye. My cousin, Marty Harrison, is an artist who brought his love of creation to the writing table. Joyce Perry ably orchestrated the chaos in the project as an editor. Many thanks to the whole team. Sometimes there were battles over details; for me, it has been worth the fight.

Through it all, my religion, the Bahá'í Faith, has been the horizon to which I turn for moral guidance and strength. It has taught me that there is only one truth—with many, diverse manifestations. It has been invaluable to my understanding of creativity and innovation. Though the list of Bahá'ís who have been dear to me (and crucial to my development) over the years is too long to write, I must especially thank the Local Spiritual Assembly of the Bahá'ís of Rochester, an institution which has changed in composition over the years, but which has always provided me with an intellectual, emotional, and moral foundation. I must also single out Dana Paxson, Jack Thatcher, Nat Rutstein, Javidukht Khadem, Ray Rouse, Robert Henderson, and Borrah Kavelin, whom I only ever met in a dream.

Finally, I need to express my gratitude to my family, my "living laboratory." When I adopted my children, it was because they needed homes. I didn't realize that they would be the ones—together with my wife's and my biological children—with the true gifts to offer. From oldest to youngest: Libby taught me about cheerful perseverance in times of intense trials; Adam's creative spark is a constant wonder; Josh's calm and his peacemaking have long been a blessing in the household; Sara, who struggles in her daily life against injustice, is an example of loyalty in friendship; Jonathan, a refugee of the Vietnam War, brings a delightful sense of humor and play into our midst; Maggie, has as keen and quiet an understanding of people as I have ever seen; and finally our youngest, Jasmine, has endlessly amazed me with her inner strength even under very difficult times. Thank you all, from the bottom of my heart.

My wife Debbie is my closest friend, my other. It is to her that I dedicate this book.

FOREWORD

*An advantage of being a child is you don't have years of
logic saying your dreams won't come true.*

—*Adam Rosenfeld (11 years old), May 4, 1982.*

I have seven children and together they have taught me
that humanity is like a garden. Each child is different;
each has his or her own talents and quirks. Five are
adopted, and among them are the mixed genes of Blacks and
Whites, and Vietnamese. All are beautiful.

My children have taught me about diversity and what it really
implies. Far more important than the superficial differences in
their colors and features, have been the differences in their
characters and personalities. Though my wife and I raised them
all together, they each blossomed and struggled in their own,
unique ways. Some children were outgoing, and others loved
the quiet of their rooms; some were wildly inquisitive, and others
could spend countless hours with a Barbie City or a collection of
racing cars. Some were more naturally obedient and others more
naturally questioning and rebellious. Every day of parenting has
brought new moments of discovery and required regular,
insistent paradigm shifts on my part.

There is no separating the lessons my children have given
me from my process of discovery around the subject of

13

innovation. I remember when I was just learning about the theory of personality types and applying them to my work. One of my daughters seemed down every day when she came home from school. She wasn't inviting her friends over to the house to play and she looked miserable while interacting with family and guests. I went to her and asked her if something was wrong. First, she hemmed and hawed. Finally, she told me that she really didn't want to offend the family by her absence, but all the people around all the time were driving her crazy. My house has always been filled with guests and friends and boarders (themselves from all different backgrounds and from all parts of the world). A bell went off in my head. I asked my daughter if she got energy from that time she spent alone. She told me she did. I realized that my daughter was a classic introvert. I later tested her and found I was right. As a strong extrovert myself (with a very extroverted lifestyle), I had earlier thought that people spent time alone only when they were down or depressed. Now I saw the situation differently. I told my daughter that the best thing she could do for the family was to rejuvenate herself by spending time in her room. Over the years, I have learned (and continue learning) how to speak to each of my children differently. Underneath this effort is the idea that there is a fundamental nobility and worth in all human beings, and that diversity must be respected and gently explored to achieve common understanding and meet goals.

Creativity in my children comes in raw, surprising, and very diverse forms. My son Adam's off-handed comment about his dreams when he was eleven years old (he is now 31 and the father of three) has been framed and put in my office. It reminds me of the innocence and openness of childhood; it reminds me that linear logic is not always the way to solve problems. It reminds me, as I work at serving a broad range of corporations, that the very structures we take for granted to get things done can become the largest obstacles to achieving our goals—since structures, by themselves, are not companies. People, in all their varieties, are the companies.

The corporate environment is made of human beings as diverse and rich, and, in their own ways, as unique and beautiful as my family of children. The corporate world, for too many of us, feels faceless and dehumanized. I have dedicated my life to wrestling with human principles that I'm convinced are universal. In this book, I sketch the journey of discovery I have made regarding these hidden, human principles. These are principles which, when applied, are at the root of the innovation process; though invisible, they bring innovation to life.

INTRODUCTION

What is innovation? Popular culture thinks it knows. An innovation is "the better mousetrap." It is the complex widget that makes a toaster run better, a computer work faster, the men and women in a spacecraft breathe easier. What is an innovator, the maker of the widget? The figure that lurks behind the better mousetrap is often thought of as wild-eyed and misunderstood, tirelessly working away in a dark basement or long-forgotten barn.

These popular conceptions have some truth in them, but they are severely limited. Innovation is more than high-tech gadgets, and innovators are complex, whole human beings of all different backgrounds and types. I propose this: An innovation is a creative act or solution that results in a quantifiable gain. An innovation is set into motion in the world of ideas, but is realized in the world of human action. Organizations need innovation like plants need water; without it, they die.

One hundred and fifty years ago, the whole planet sat in candle-lit darkness at night. A century ago, the first scratchy sounds of radio echoed in the silence of the ether, forever linking large populations together. Fifty years ago, the surface of the moon was still the object of poetry, not yet of scientific exploration. Ten years ago, the world barely knew the Internet that today links my office in Rochester, New York, to a Zambian village. We live in a world of technological change, where newness clamors as it speeds by. This ephemeral aspect of life is critical to our survival and to our realization as a human race.

At the same time, our economy is inextricably bound to this process. Businesses react to and generate change, at ever-increasing rates. But as important as the dynamic of newness and invention is, it would be a mistake to think that all the methods of business are subject to the same law of change. In my 25 years of experience in and around the business of ideas, I've realized that there are constants that come in the form of operational principles—principles that relate to the relationship between people and ideas. Technologies change. People change. The paradox is that without applying timeless principles, the culture of change cannot endure. It is because of the timeless nature of the principles in my book that I deliberately omitted references to contemporary journals and resources. Instead, I've drawn examples from a wide variety of sources—from both inside and outside the business world, and from both current news and historic records. As you will see, these examples solidify the universality and timelessness of the innovation principles discussed throughout the book.

Another important point to make is that sustaining innovation depends on the human beings who make it happen. I have found that to foster and sustain the creative spirit, an organization must understand and act in accordance with the human principles that underlie the innovation process. Understanding these principles requires an honest focus on people and their relationship with business and organizational concerns. Whether you work in the corporate world, a governmental or municipal agency, an academic institution, or the not-for-profit sector, these same principles still apply. This is because only human beings create ideas; only human beings can sow the seeds of innovation. In this book, it is my hope to show how focusing on people—their unique qualities, their values, and their diverse organizational roles—is the most essential step in creating a vibrant, flourishing, innovating organization.

While it is true, then, that business and technology play a critical role in the innovation process, the human element is the driving force. It can be said that the "right people" in an organization are its greatest asset; the wrong people are its greatest liability. Studies have shown, in fact, that the quality of a work force may, over time, be more important to a company's stock offering than its technology (see Figure 0.1).

Figure 0.1: The Impact of the Human Element on IPOs

Factor	Date of IPO	3 Years Later
Technology	1	5
Rewards	2	4
Product	3	3
Management	4	2
Employees	5	1

Cornell Study of IPOs (Factors affecting stock prices)   1 = High Impact; 5 = Low Impact
Theresa M. Welbourne, Ph. D.

Of the top five factors affecting the stock price of an initial public offering (IPO), the company's technology has the strongest impact. Quality of employees is fifth. Three years later, the people of the company (employees and management) have the strongest effect on the stock price and, of the top five factors, technology has the least effect. Re-printed with permission from Theresa M. Welbourne, Ph.D.

Making the Invisible Visible is organized around the human principles I have identified—each chapter highlighting a single principle. The book is divided into two parts, with Part I relating to the "essence" of the innovation process and Part II relating to the "environment" of the innovation process. It was said of poet Edgar Allen Poe that he had "a small steam engine in the brain, which not only (set) the cerebral mass in motion but (kept) the owner in hot water."[1] In the course of the book, I show that ideas do not propel themselves; the passion behind an idea is what ultimately drives innovations to conclusion. It is essential for managers to understand how passionate enthusiasm plays a role in the workplace and to protect those who have it from both themselves and others.

Part II of the book focuses on the human environment that surrounds the creation of ideas that lead to innovation. Perhaps especially relevant during this time of Enron and World-Com are the discussions in Chapter 7, which concerns the destructive elements that are present at the creation of an organization. For easy reference, I have included at the end of the book a set of appendices that provide chapter summary points, a glossary of innovation terms, a detailed description of five different innovation systems, and a look at an idea's journey through the innovation process.

On the whole, Making the Invisible Visible sets forth principles that are necessary to create an innovative culture and help innovation leaders find and nurture the right people. Many studies look at the visible results of operating methods of organizations, but I believe that the principles behind them are so deceptively simple that they are taken for granted or overlooked.

I admit that I have a weakness for watching ideas being born. And I have a weakness for the people who develop ideas and the processes that bring ideas to fruition. These people come in all forms, colors, tones and temperaments— from the dazzling to the meditative, from the studious to the raucous. I've had the great luck to do a lot of laughing over the years with the cast of characters around me—some of whom do look a lot like those wild-eyed basement dwellers! The simple joy of "idea play" first attracted me to

---

[1]   *New York Weekly Mirror*, July 5, 1845

the field of innovation. But I have grown to understand, in all seriousness, how vitally important it is. This book, then, is about serious play and timeless change. It is for managers, innovation leaders, or anyone inspired by a love of actualized ideas.

CHAPTER 1

The Human Component
In A Changing World

Nothing endures but change.

—*Heraclitus (c. 500 B.C.), Greek philosopher.*

What do Ford, Delta, Disney, Hewlett-Packard, *Reader's Digest*, and Barbie dolls have in common? They all had their starts in garages. More than that, Henry Ford, C. E. Woolman, Walt Disney, David Packard, Hewlett, DeWitt and Lila Wallace, Ruth and Elliot Handler, and "Matt" Matson all had exciting ideas, faced skeptics and opposition, and had little financial backing, but had faith in what they were doing, courage, and persistence. All of them were people of vision who had a passion for pursuing their ideas, putting them on the leading edge of change. They were innovators. They made changes that made a difference.

Some of the great innovations in history have been instantly understood and accepted. Others have required a long and sometimes arduous journey toward refinement and public appreciation. We often take for granted the technological advancements that are ever present in our modern world and we don't consider the historical twists and turns that allowed the idea to flourish. The fax is a good example of how an idea developed slowly and with the participation of many thinkers and players.[2] As early as 1840 (yes, 1840!), Alexander Bain, a watchmaker from Scotland, wondered about a way to send pictures to distant places. He thought of using wires for transmission, and in 1843 patented the forerunner of the fax. It was a big, cumbersome device that used a pendulum—after all, Bain was a watchmaker. In addition to its nearly six-foot-high size, there was a major problem of synchronizing the sending and receiving signals so they would appear on the same place on a page. A few years later, Frederick Bakewell improved the system by using a rotating drum and stylus. Later a priest, Giovanni Caselli, made further improvements so that sending and receiving were better synchronized. This made the device commercially practical.

Emperor Napoleon III a tinkerer himself, was impressed. For five years during the 1870s there were official transmissions (then called the pentelegraph) between Lyons and Paris, France. The Franco-Prussian war ended the reign of Napoleon III. It also ended distance transmission, a casualty of politics and war. But the concept did not die. The pentelegraph was neither commercially successful, nor forgotten. Other improvements were made with a long parade of innovators who inched the development forward. Among others playing a role in its development were Willoughby Smith in 1873, G. R. Carey in 1875, Noah Amstutz in 1891, Arthur Korn in 1902, and Édouard Belin in 1913.

By 1924, the device was sufficiently practical that Western Union used wire facsimiles to send photographs to newspapers.

---

[2]   See Bill Yenne, Morton, Dr. Grosser, ed., *100 Inventions that Shaped World History*, Bluewood Books, San Mateo, California, 1993; also see Donald G. Fink, *Facsimile*, Vol. 9, Colliers Encyclopedia CD-ROM, 02-28-1996.

But there was still a major problem limiting greater use—the problem was language. Machines made by one manufacturer could not "talk to" or interface with equipment made by others. The big breakthrough came in 1974 when the United Nations established a universal facsimile language. Once the language problem was solved, it didn't take long for the fax to become an essential part of the business world. By the late 1970s, a century after the fax had been used in France, courier companies were installing the machines in their offices. Soon, large companies bypassed courier companies by installing fax machines in their major offices. This increased the demand for machines, driving down prices. The fax machine's seemingly sudden appearance was more than a century and a half after the first patent. It was made possible by the long, unnoticed, series of technological developments and the 1974 standardization of language and transmission modes. Today the fax machine is commonplace and taken for granted.

Change is not always welcome. A graphic designer in New York wanted his clients in different cities to get fax machines for ease of transmitting sketches and seeing work in progress. Instead of applauding the idea, some opposed it. He almost lost one client, who became irate and accused the designer of hustling him into buying equipment he didn't need. The man thought the designer must have been getting a kickback. Why else suggest such an outlandish thing? In just a few years, however, fax machines seemed to appear everywhere.

The final development of the fax machine is a good metaphor for the vital importance of a universal language and a common core of concepts within the field of innovation. How can there be a significant advance in any field without a common nomenclature as a means to exchange basic information? What is chemistry without the periodic table and standardized units of weights and measurement, or maritime travel without a universally recognized communications code? In 1857 the British Board of Trade published a communications code using 18 flags for 70,000 messages giving ships at sea greatly improved communications.[3] Sir Francis Bacon (1561-1626) is considered the father of modern science[4] because he introduced several ideas for common understanding. His reasoning became the basis for achieving objectivity, detachment, and the use of empirical evidence. Another key historic figure is Samuel Morse, who did more for technology than invent the telegraph. He demonstrated digital language. That concept is the heart of computer language.

What does all this have to do with innovation? Today the field of innovation is floundering for several reasons. First, the field does not have a universally accepted core of concepts, or principles. Until this book, the principles that underlie the human elements of innovations have not been spelled out. Second, there is the matter of nomenclature. Not only does every company have its own set of terms, but different departments within organizations also use different names for the same thing, which makes communications difficult. It is almost like a 21st century Tower of Babel wherein people with similar ideas have difficulty communicating. The Glossary in Appendix B is designed to attempt to standardize the vocabulary. In addition to the lack of universally accepted principles and inconsistent nomenclature within the field of innovation, the human component of ideas is crucial. The consequences of human neglect cannot be overstated, because it is the human element that makes the whole idea system work.

Ideas are a dime a dozen. People who put them into action are priceless.

—Author Unknown

---

[3]   "International Code of Signals," *Microsoft® Encarta® 97 Encyclopedia*, 1997.

[4]   "Bacon, Francis, 1st Baron Verulam and Viscount Saint Albans," *Microsoft Encarta 97 Encyclopedia*, 1997.

There are three interconnected components of a successful enterprise: business, technical and human. The human component binds the other two components together and makes the whole system work. I looked for a way to illustrate this complex interrelationship and the model that seemed to fit best was the DNA double helix, as illustrated in Figure 1.1.

Figure 1.1: The Innovation Model

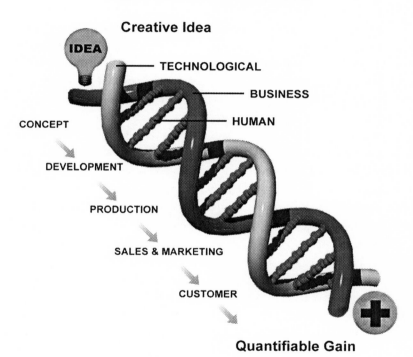

All ideas have both business and technological dimensions. The human dynamics of innovation is the invisible life force that holds it together.

One strand of the helix represents the technological component of innovation within an enterprise. For example, at Eastman Kodak, the technological component of my work was the production of liquid crystals, silver halide chemistry, silicon wafers, photovoltaics, and so on. The second strand represents the business aspect of enterprise, including all the complexities of developmental costs, venture capital, promotion, market acceptance, production costs, break-even points, and so on. Connecting the two strands of the helix is the human component. The helix, which could be called the "genetic code" of an organization, shows how these elements are intertwined. Just as living organisms have genetic codes, so too, the interplay among the three affect each other, shape the corporate culture, and determine long-term strengths and weaknesses. These genes are the invisible people principles.

Innovation thrives in environments in which the three components are integrated in a healthy way. Executives in successful companies know that a constant flow of new ideas is needed for their companies to stay healthy, yet few have recognized the importance of the interplay of the three components of innovation. Even fewer are aware that a huge reservoir of ideas is lying dormant in every organization. This resource is largely invisible. Rarely do companies find a way to evaluate and make use of the best of these ideas, but once discovered and tapped, this reservoir can provide undreamed of benefits.

Twenty-five years ago, while working for Eastman Kodak Company, I noticed that people at all levels within the company had ideas that could benefit both themselves and the company. They knew the business, its culture, and its needs. Their day-to-day, hands-on experience gave them insights that were hard to match. What's more, many of them were deeply committed to the organization. A few of these ideas found a supportive ear, but most of them did not. The successful ones usually fit conveniently into the company's existing structure. Other good ideas did not, so they languished. I was convinced that if there were some way to infuse these ideas into the organization, they would be of value to the company. It was a serious problem and the company was losing out on some potentially major benefits.

Why was this? The company wanted ideas, and employees had ideas they wanted to share. Why weren't they connecting? Several factors contributed to the problem:

- There was no effective way to talk about the innovation process
- Even though the company solicited ideas and had a documented innovation process, that process worked best for small, incremental changes. The mechanism to make use of spontaneous new products, breakthrough ideas, or anything that seemed unusual was inadequate.
- Each department and each division built for itself a subculture that was different from the rest of the organization. This internal structuring was like building walls that insulated each department from others.
- The environment was suited to the comfortable and the status quo. There was little room or tolerance for anyone with wildly different ideas and behaviors.
- A structure was needed based on bonds of trust, confidence, and respect for those involved. It would have to encourage individuals with unusual ideas and cut across departmental boundaries.

In short, a mechanism was needed for idea connections. There were others in the company who saw the same need and we worked together to find a way to address the problem. The solution was the establishment of the first Office of Innovation. The challenges and frustrations of setting up the office were monumental, but it would take another book to tell the whole story. It is enough to say that persistence, blood, sweat, and tears opened and sustained the Office of Innovation. Many individuals took risks to make it happen, notably Bob Bacon, Tom Whitely, and Bob Tuite. The Office of Innovation gave individuals a safe haven in which to bring forth ideas and develop them. Promising ones received serious attention and a few were highly successful.

That is how I got started in the field of innovation, which has been my "professional" life now for more than twenty years. In those early days, not much had been written on the subject. Innovation was an unknown word and I felt as if I were walking down an unfamiliar country road at night without a light or a map. It has been a journey of trial and a lot of error—and, ultimately, a journey of tremendous satisfaction.

As more and more people understood the importance of innovation, I was asked to help other companies set up innovation systems based on the model at Kodak. I was happy to comply. What I found, however, was that while the offices started out successfully, over time they tended to lose their effectiveness. This was puzzling and distressing. If the system was sound, and I was convinced it was, why wasn't it working as it should? Something was missing. Then I realized that I had concentrated so heavily on the mechanics of setting up offices and making them operational that essential components were over-looked:

- One crucial element was the need for sustained *commitment at a high level* within the company. New processes have to overcome an enormous amount of inertia while established ones often outlive their usefulness. A high-ranking officer in the company needs to understand the difficulties involved and be committed to the ongoing and long-term success of the program. Lacking that, it will fail no matter how much compelling evidence is produced to show its value.
- It is essential to *operate on a people-based level.* That sounds simple, but requires more than lip service or superficial understanding and application.
- *Sustaining innovation is based on underlying principles* that are not readily apparent. To become successful, the invisible must be made visible.

What I had done was give companies the form or structure, but not enough education on its spirit or soul. Ironically, I was violating one of my cardinal rules. I was working on the level of method rather than underlying principle. Until then, I had not realized how subtle and difficult it is to communicate the principles. As one musician said when asked to define jazz, "If you have to ask, you'll never know."

In this book, stories and illustrations are used to convey the soul or spirit of sustaining innovation, while at the same time explaining the principles. A principle, as used in this book for the concept of innovation, is defined as a **fundamental and timeless natural law that underlies the methods and techniques used to sustain innovation.**

A major distinction between principles and methods is that principles are timeless, methods change. From a technical standpoint, whether you are talking about a horse and buggy or an automobile, a means is needed to control speed. A hundred years ago, all it took was a buggy whip, reins and sometimes brakes. Today, for automobiles, accelerator pedals and brakes are used. Some day, the accelerator pedal will go the way of the buggy whip. Yet, the principle will remain the same. Some new method will be devised to control the speed of vehicles. The buggy whip, the accelerator pedal, and whatever is next are the means of applying the principle according to the technology and circumstances of the time. People in all fields, from accounting to engineering to graphic arts, use principles that are timeless even though technology has drastically altered the way they are applied. It is hard to find ledger books, slide rulers, or French curves anymore, but the underlying principles have not changed.

A century ago, a man with a business could almost guarantee that his son would be able to take over the business and run it the way his father had, simply by using the same methods. Today, the increasing rate of rapid global changes, business practices, technology, and geo-political conditions make such a simple transition in running a successful business impossible. The son or daughter would be able to maintain the business only if he or she understood that it was the principles behind the methods that were responsible for the business' success, not the methods themselves. If the father's methods were applied without understanding their underlying principles, then the business would not be successful—it could even fail. Methods change; principles endure. Principles are deceptively simple. They can, therefore, be taken for granted or over-looked. Results are visible and receive the most notice and attention. Some methods and actions are also visible, although some are not. Principles are almost always invisible. But, results depend on the unseen principles. Operating on methods, without regard to underlying principles, causes problems. Some are obvious and some are not. Obvious or not, they cause downward spirals that can destroy a company. It is hard to work consistently on the level of principle, especially when it appears that our methods are working well. The following diagram (Figure 1.2) illustrates the relationship between principles, methods/activities and results.

Figure 1.2: Timeless Source of Results

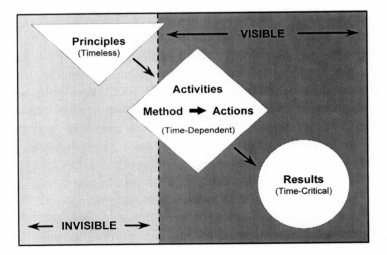

Most principles are invisible. Some of the methods and actions are also invisible. Results are visible and receive the most notice and attention.

The visible parts receive attention and are frequent topics at conferences, workshops, and internal training sessions. The underlying principles are rarely mentioned.

In order for the invisible parts to become a normal part of your thinking, start at the back of this book. Look at Appendix A: Summary (p. 185) and Appendix E: Innovation Workbook (p. 221). Before reading each chapter, I recommend you read the summary and workbook exercises. This prepares your mind by focusing on what I think are the most significant things for you to gain. Then, read and enjoy the chapter. These ideas will become more firmly embedded in your thinking.

It is time to look at the principles one by one, starting with the problems. Why problems? Because innovations start when problems are converted into ideas.

PART I

The Innovation Process:
Its Essence

Sustaining innovation is a process with many components interacting in a dynamic and energizing way.

In the following chapters I discuss five principles of innovation that combine to give life to the process. They are illustrated in a variety of ways to show that principles are timeless, but methods need to be modified according to the time and situation.

- Innovation Starts When People Convert Problems Into Ideas.
- Innovation Needs a System.
- Passion Is the Fuel and Pain Is the Hidden Ingredient.
- Co-Locate for Effective Exchange.
- Leverage Differences.

These are discussed individually although they are interrelated, interdependent, and all play essential roles in the innovation process.

There is a direct relationship between how well these principles are applied and the ability of the innovation leader to sustain the innovation process within the organization.

CHAPTER 2

Innovation Starts When People Convert Problems Into Ideas

Anything one man can imagine, other men can make real.

—Jonathan Swift (1667-1745),
English writer and satirist.

New ideas are born through questions, problems, and obstacles. The process of innovation is indebted to the trouble that comes about when we are surrounded by that which is not solved, not smooth, and not simple. Therefore, in order for the innovation process to flourish, it needs a climate that encourages inquiry and welcomes problems. This is not always easy (and is certainly counter-intuitive at times), but it is the only way for ideas to be set into motion and, eventually, to be transformed into quantifiable gains.

Civilization was born with fire. About 25,000 years ago, someone saw the advantage of fires occurring in nature and wondered about controlling them and using them deliberately. Nobody knows how many problems and false starts there were as early man struggled with making fire, a breakthrough that has been called the most important tool in the development of civilization.

There is another piece to the story. It was probably the beginning of innovation: wondering about things and experimenting until something different or better was produced. With the new tool of fire and the birth of innovation, the journey of an ever-advancing civilization began.

As early as the second century A.D., the Greek satirist Lucian wondered about the moon and wrote about an imaginary lunar voyage.[5] The technological advances after World War II moved the subject from questions and dreams to the threshold of achievement. In 1961, President John F. Kennedy announced the ambitious goal of putting a man on the moon before the end of the decade[6] and in July 1969, Neal Armstrong gave reality to the dream. But first came the question illuminating the problem, which led to a host of ideas that burned in the hearts and minds of dreamers for centuries until the day of fulfillment.

Other ideas spring from a perceived need. Who was the first person who wondered about getting to the other side of a lake or a river? Today we go over or under water by boats, bridges, and tunnels without giving it a second thought. That is possible because someone questioned, dreamed, schemed, and experimented until ways were found to get to the other side.

Sometimes a product's conception is incidental to another problem being solved. Alexander Graham Bell arrived in the United States in 1871 and began teaching

---

[5]   "Lucian," *Microsoft Encarta 97 Encyclopedia*, 1997.

[6]   Von Braun and Ordway, "Apollo Program," *Encyclopedia Americana*, 2000, vol. 25, pp. 381-383.

deaf-mutes, using a system similar to today's lip-reading.[7] But Bell was not satisfied. He wanted more and wondered if there was some way to amplify sound so the hard-of-hearing could enjoy its benefits. His concept grew far beyond the question he raised. He ended up with a telephone and made an unsuccessful attempt to sell his invention to Western Union. They could see no future for what they considered to be a toy. Instead of being put off, Bell pursued its application himself and his telephone gained recognition at the 1876 Centennial Exposition in Philadelphia. This led to the organization of the Bell Telephone Company in 1877.

Some problems are answered quickly. Others remain for a long time, generating a myriad of ideas before a practical solution is found. Flight is a good example. One of the earliest inventors to design a helicopter was Leonardo da Vinci (1452-1519). In one of his notebooks from 1480, da Vinci illustrated a model helicopter driven by a clockwork motor. His notes imply that the model flew, but there is no verification.[8] When an idea affects someone so profoundly that finding answers becomes an obsession, persistence and removing great obstacles often follow. The Wright brothers were obsessed by what had been a dream for da Vinci. Years were spent on a diligent, disciplined, and frustrating search for a way to fly. In 1903 they succeeded with the first manned, powered flight at Kitty Hawk, North Carolina.[9] The centuries-old riddle of flight had at last been solved, and the solution became a defining feature of the 20th century. Once again, a question had framed a problem—and passion for a solution led to the ideas and innovations that produced results.

Some advances taken for granted today, like the fax described in the preceding chapter, were developed only after

7   "Bell, Alexander Graham," *Microsoft Encarta 97 Encyclopedia*, 1997.

8   "History of the Helicopter," *Microsoft Encarta Reference Library*, 2002.

9   "Kitty Hawk," Ibid.

an incredibly long list of people posed questions and sought answers. Consider something as ordinary as a modern table; the process of its development has been long and complex. Perhaps it began with a cave dweller who found an elevated flat surface to be useful and wondered if something like that could be built. Later someone attached legs to a flat object. As the centuries passed, many thinkers developed the myriad materials and designs that can be used for a table. The result is today's sophisticated process, including designing, manufacturing, finishing, packaging, shipping, marketing, and finally the transportation that brings a table to your house. It would be impossible to list all the innovations that were a part of the table's story, but this much is certain: before each innovation, there was an idea spawned by the question, "Is there a better or a different way to do this?"

Problems precede questions, which precede the thoughts that generate ideas. All this happens in the minds of people who are driven to find answers. What are ideas anyway? Definitions range from "a vague notion or impression" to "an opinion or belief" to "a plan for action." I think of an idea as a **mental concept or image**.

Once the question is properly framed and understood,
the solution is often self-evident.

The Source of Ideas

Ideas come from people. They come from people searching for answers to questions or problems. Where do people get their ideas? Suffice it to say that we all have billions of bits of information inside of us. When combined in new and unusual ways, ideas are formed. The capacity for generating ideas varies from the person who has few ideas and "can't think of anything" to the one who has such a flood of ideas that she can't stop generating new ones. This is a style of thinking and should not be confused with ability or intelligence.

Graham Wallas[10] discovered and listed four stages in his model of the creative process. His model is timeless and has been true throughout history.

1. The first stage, *preparation*, features a thorough investigation into the problem, then gathering relevant information and phrasing the question properly. The importance of this is often overlooked. Some people spend 10% of their time trying to understand the problem and 90% coming up with solutions. For others 90% of the time is spent thinking about the problem and 10% devoted to solution. In my observations, the latter group generally comes up with the best answers.
2. Wallas' second stage is *incubation*. It is a period of time when one takes a break from the problem. Many people maintain this is the time when the unconscious mind takes over to work on the problem.
3. The third stage, *illumination*, is a flash where things that were not connected suddenly come together, sometimes called the moment of "Aha!"
4. In the fourth stage, *validation*, the flash of insight is tried out in ways that can be verified.

This model has a built-in problem for many managers. Both the preparation and the incubation stages follow their own time schedules. Trying to rush them may or may not work. Managers who think linearly are time-driven and have difficulty with anything that cannot be placed in a predictable time slot. Some ideas are stimulated by external sources and some seem to come from within, with no known external connection. There are also ideas that come from the interaction of two or more people. All of these go through the stages described by Wallas.

---

[10]   Graham Wallas, *The Art of Thought*, Harcourt, New York, 1926.

External stimuli.

George de Mestra (1907-1990) was taking a stroll in his native Switzerland. Like many hikers, he returned home with a jacket full of cockleburs. Other hikers had encountered this pesky nuisance and painstakingly removed the burs, one at a time, but de Mestral took it a step further. He wondered why they stuck, put them under his microscope for a careful look, and noticed tiny hooks that had entangled themselves in the loops of his jacket's fabric. That would be enough to satisfy most people's curiosity, but not de Mestral's. He wondered if nature's hooks could be duplicated so that things could be stuck together on purpose and be pulled apart fairly easily. Fabrics were developed in France and given the name Velcro, a combination of velvet and crochet.[11] Good things happen when preparedness and opportunity meet. In the 1950s, the concept of space travel created new needs. One of them was how to keep things from floating around in-side a space capsule. Velcro came to the rescue. This usage popularized the product and made Velcro universal.

Internal stimuli.

Friedrick Kekulé (1829-1896), a world-renowned chemist, was puzzled about the nature of organic compounds. He spent hours pondering the question and it became a recurring theme in his dreams until his dreams led him to a flash of insight. Commenting on the illuminating dream, he said, "I turned my chair to the fire and dozed. Again the atoms were gamboling before my eyes. This time the smaller groups kept modestly in the background. My mental eye, rendered more acute by repeated visions of this kind, could now distinguish larger

---

[11]   For details on the origins of Velcro®, see Charles Panati, *Panati's Extraordinary Origins of Everyday Things*, Harper & Row, New York.

structures, of manifold conformation; long rows, sometimes more closely fitted together; all twining and twisting in snakelike motion. But look! What was that? One of the snakes had seized hold of its own tail, and the form whirled mockingly before my eyes. As if by the flash of lighting I awoke." That insight led to the idea that the carbon chain of the organic compound benzene was ring-shaped. This opened up a whole new way of thinking about organic chemistry and is the basis for how it is understood today. Kekulé concluded the statement of discovery with some good advice: "Let us learn to dream, gentlemen."[12]

Occasionally, one person will have an idea and independently push it through to a conclusion. The invention of the zipper is a good example. In this case there was nothing but the determination of one man, Whitcomb Judson (1846-1909).[13] His friends said that all you had to do was say to Judson, "I wish there were a way to do this or that," and Judson would find a way to do it. He had a friend with a bad back, which gave him excruciating pain when he leaned over to tie his shoes. According to legend, Judson wondered if he could invent a fastener that his friend could use without hurting his back. From there Judson went to his shop. Inspired to relieve the pain and suffering of his friend, he used the principle of sprockets of a bicycle and the idea of a hook and eye. He then developed the prototype of a zipper—so called because things could be fastened in a "zip." He took the full journey from idea to the quantifiable gain to help his friend. And, he did it alone and unaided.

[12] Friedrich Kekulé, cited in Arthur Koestler's *The Act of Creation*, Macmillan, New York, 1964, p. 118.

[13] From D. Buchman and S. Groves, *What If? Fifty Discoveries that Changed the World*, Scholastic, Inc, New York, 1988, p. 42. Also, for an in-depth look at the invention of the zipper, see Robert Friedel, *Zipper: An Exploration in Novelty*, Norton, New York. Also see Charles Panati, op. cit.

Group stimuli.

More often, however, group stimulation is involved. This is direct and simple. When two or more people come together with an attitude of trust and mutual respect, and work on a common problem, they stimulate each other. As I mentioned earlier, new ideas are formed when two or more bits of unconnected information are combined. When a subject comes up, one person may have four ideas and another one has five. If they share their thoughts in an atmosphere of trust and amity, they stimulate new ideas in each other. The result is that 4 plus 5 does not equal 9, but a dozen, or 20, or 100 or more. As thoughts are shared, they become refined and shaped into something newer and better than any of the individual contributions.[14] The work of Alex Osborn (1888-1966)[15] has made the term "brain storming" popular all over the world. The term has become generic and is often used when people get together to generate ideas, whether or not they use Osborn's model.

Many innovations today are the result of what could be called a "relay race" of team efforts. In this process, several people are involved in the different phases of bringing an idea to fruition. Interestingly, the people involved are often completely unaware of the role (or even existence) of the others in the process. When I was at Kodak, a security guard had an idea about making a new security badge. At about the same time, a chemical engineer had a piece of material for which he was hoping to find an interesting use. Both men presented their ideas to the Office of Innovation (see Chapter 3), but they didn't go very far. Later, a major international project came up that required tight security. The two ideas were

---

[14]   John Kolstoe, *Developing Genius*, George Ronald, Oxford, 1995, Appendix A.

[15]   Alex F. Osborn, *Applied Imagination*, 3rd rev. ed., Charles Scribner's Sons, New York, 1963.

recalled, combined, and a new product was developed. The people who finally brought this idea to its conclusion had no idea of the original source. After the project was completed, I had the 25 key people who had worked on the project come together in one large room. They were lined up according to the order in which they had done their work. The two originators of the idea—the security guard and the chemical engineer—were placed at the head of the line. Everyone was asked if they knew the people standing ahead of them and behind them. They all did. Many also knew the chemical engineer. But, no one knew the security guard, let alone the fact that he had been an initiator of the project.

Importance of new ideas in business

I think of organizations as living, breathing organisms in a constant state of renewal. Fresh ideas leading to innovations are like oxygen. Getting sufficient oxygen means breathing in and exhaling a large volume of air to extract the needed oxygen. In the same way, incorporating good ideas into the workings of an organization means examining a large number that will not work. But, like oxygen, the flow of ideas is essential for an organization to maintain health, vigor, and viability.

Studies have shown a direct relationship between a company's position in industry and the number of new products introduced within the last five years. Albert Page, Professor of Marketing at the University of Illinois at Chicago and a leading researcher and author on new product development, made a presentation to the Product Development and Management Association in Chicago in 1991. According to his findings, leaders in industries obtained nearly half of their sales revenue from products that had been introduced in the past five years. Those in the bottom third of their respective industries averaged little more than 10% of their sales from products introduced in the past five years. Figure 2.1 shows this relationship.

Figure 2.1: Industry Position/Sales
from Products Comparison

Position of Firm in Its Industry	Percent of Sales from Products Introduced in the Last 5 Years
Leader in Industry	49.1
Top Third of Industry	33.8
Middle Third of Industry	26.9
Bottom Third of Industry	10.7

Albert L. Page, University of Illinois, Chicago. Presentation to Product Development & Management Association, Chicago, November 13, 1991.

The leading company in an industry has the largest percentage of its sales from products introduced in the last five years. Reprinted with permission from Albert L. Page.

The lesson is simple. Companies with the most new products and/or services are the firms that prosper and grow. The companies that produce the fewest new products and services do not perform as well, and are in the lower tier for their industries.

But there is an even greater, underlying lesson. While superficially obvious, it is not well understood: *all new products and services come from ideas and all ideas come from people who are stimulated, motivated, and encouraged in specific ways.*

Planned and Unplanned Ideas

Innovations can be divided between planned and unplanned. There are some characteristic differences between them. Planned innovations are part of the normal management strategy of setting a course for a company's future direction. Many are in response to specific problems or challenges. Companies plan innovations as a normal part of business in order to improve existing products or processes in a systematic manner.

Compared to the planned innovations, however, the origins and development of the unplanned tend to be untidy, erratic, and unpredictable. Mistakes, failures, and false starts have been the basis of a whole host of innovations—but, as Bell discovered, so has serendipity, where one thing was sought and something else found. Likewise, idle curiosity, chance ideas, and creative inspiration have been rich sources of unplanned ideas.

Sometimes a concept will be around for a long time, but only partially developed. It may be a short step away from a major breakthrough, even though the creator does not know it. DuPont scientist William Carothers (1896-1937) was trying to develop synthetic fibers using polymers and heat.[16] There were no successes and by the middle of 1933 fiber research came to a halt. So, Carothers literally put his product on the shelf without even bothering to patent it and turned his attention to other matters. Later, he became the head of the laboratory where Julian Hill worked. Out of simple curiosity, Hill was fooling around with the product Carothers had shelved. Hill discovered that when he stuck a glass stirring rod into the beaker of the polyester and pulled it out, it would stretch into long, silky strands, thinner than a spider's thread, without breaking. Up to that time, heat had been used to draw out polyesters. No one thought of "cold drawing," such as using the glass stirring rod to pull out the polyester, until Hill fooled around with the idea. One day, while Carothers was gone, the lab workers expanded the fun. They decided to see how far they could stretch the polyester. They were delightfully surprised to find they could stretch it, without breaking, the full length of the hall. The act of cold drawing and stretching the substance actually strengthened it. With that new

---

[16]   D. Buchman and S. Groves, *What If? Fifty Discoveries that Changed the World,* Scholastic, Inc., New York, 1988, p. 42.

knowledge, work resumed on the product. The idea had lain dormant, but playful curiosity gave new life to this product now called nylon. There is another important distinction: the difference between innovations that are incremental, minor changes in the way something works or is produced, and breakthrough innovations. Breakthrough innovations have a major impact. The use of a ballpoint pen was a breakthrough innovation for writing instruments. Improving the ink flow and the looks of the pen are incremental changes.

Studies from Japan to Europe[17] have confirmed that most planned innovations are incremental and that most of the really big ones that make a major difference are unplanned. Successful companies spend a lot of time and money planning and developing ideas. However, few companies have good methods for stimulating and developing unplanned ideas. Even in those organizations where an effort is made to use unplanned ideas, there are severe limitations. A major hurdle is that many people will not come forward with their ideas for fear of rejection, ridicule, getting into trouble, or having ideas stolen and developed by someone else.

The real question for any organization is two-fold: how do you find potentially useful ideas that are over and beyond those generated by existing systems, and how do you bring them to fruition? The answer to both these questions is especially challenging because unplanned ideas are usually not related to the work people are doing, or their assigned responsibilities. Ideas may be in vast supply, but there needs to be a regular means to retrieve these ideas if an organization is to benefit from them.

The innovation process can be compared to the components of a water system with a source, a method of delivery, and outlets. All three must be in good working order or else there

---

[17]   See: Sam Stern, *The Relationship Between Resource Development and Corporate Creativity in Japan*, 1992, and Rolf Berth, Senior Fellow of International Management Instate in Geneva, 1986.

will be no water where it is needed. The water system for New York City serves as a good analogy. Its source consists of reservoirs located about 80 miles away in the Catskill Mountains. There is more than enough water in the mountains to take care of the city's needs. Within an organization, the vast idea "reservoir" resides in (and is refreshed by) the people inside the company.

The second part of the water system is a means of getting the water from the mountains to the city. For New York City, huge pipes are used—some big enough to hold a truck. There are also pipes throughout the city that make up the vital, unseen link between the water in the reservoir and the ultimate user. For a company, an innovation infrastructure is the piping system through which the flow of ideas can move and develop. Today, in most organizations, this vital link is non-existent for the largest idea reservoir of all.

The third and final part of the system is the faucets, or outlets. When there is a problem with the water system in New York City and no water comes out of a faucet, where do people look to find out what's wrong? No one asks if the reservoirs are dried up. They know there is plenty of water at the source. As long as water is coming out of the pipes, people tend not to worry about whether or not the pipe is leaking or properly attached to the reservoir. In comparison, among organizations looking for ideas, even those companies that are good about tapping some reservoirs do not have a good record for recognizing and tapping the largest source of all—the ocean of ideas that come from people within the company. Profitability can mask the fact that there may be a poor connection to the best reservoir because when the company enjoys good profits, there is less incentive to look for new sources of ideas.

The data uncovered by Albert Page (as shown in Figure 2.1) is worth serious consideration. Profitable or not, if half the profits are not coming from goods or services developed during the past five years, the company may be headed toward financial problems.

The issue for companies goes beyond profitability and having a sufficient number of ideas. Rather, the issue is having a system for getting ideas from their vast, hidden, and untapped source that is found in the minds and hearts of employees at all levels of the organization and in all departments. The Office of Innovation at Kodak uniquely tapped a part of a huge reservoir of ideas hidden deep inside the company. As the office became established, it stimulated even more novel thinking, some of which led to breakthrough ideas. Employees began to feel a level of excitement, because they had a place to take their ideas. This excitement carried over to their normal work. Those who submitted ideas outside their everyday focus also became more effective in their assigned work: productivity soared. It was a double bonus for the company.

Managing Ideas

Starting with an understanding that problems, rightly considered, lead to fresh ideas, an innovation leader locates, stimulates, and encourages fresh ideas. She has to have a burning passion for finding the ideas, wherever they originate, and making sure the ideas and their creators receive proper support. She also creates an environment that stimulates ideas, encouraging everyone to ask questions and explore new problems. It takes a sincere appreciation of people who can convert problems into ideas. Such a leader understands, deeply and fully, that people who are encouraged to come forward with their ideas become the most valuable asset within a company. They are not just employees; they are the right people.

It's easy to think, "So what? What happens if I don't bother with all this stuff?" The city water system does not work unless the pipes are kept in good repair. By the same token, an organization sooner or later suffers if the idea pipes aren't in good working order. In short, if you don't sustain innovation, it's terminal. The organization dies!

While the innovation leader may know the value of people in the process, how people can convert problems into ideas, and the many forms it should take, it takes much more to foster innovation successfully. Innovation requires a support system within which the innovation process can develop.

CHAPTER 3

Innovation Needs A System

The most important, and indeed the truly unique, contribution of management in the 20th century was the fifty-fold increase in the productivity of the MANUAL WORKER in manufacturing. The most important contribution management needs to make in the 21st century is similarly to increase the productivity of KNOWLEDGE WORK and the KNOWLEDGE WORKER.

—Peter Drucker (1909-), author and consultant on strategy and policy for top management, businesses and non-profits.

All organizations have innovation systems. Some are formal, designed by the leadership, and some are informal, taking place outside established channels. Informal channels are untidy and inefficient, yet innovation is always associated with them. These channels are brimming with more potentially useful ideas than ever are used because few receive serious attention. The Originator-assisted system is described in this chapter both to show how the rich reservoir of concepts trapped in the informal system can be liberated and become a regular part of the organization's ongoing quest for new and improved products and procedures, and to illustrate the steps and difficulties of pushing an idea through.

Over the years of working in this field, I have found only five systems. They are described in Appendix C, and are listed below:

1. **Originator-assisted**, a process that helps employees transform their own ideas into business opportunities.
2. **Targeted Innovation**, a process for developing solutions to meet a specific need.
3. **Internal Venturing,** a launching process for new businesses that do not fit the company's current lines of business.
4. **Continuous Improvement**, a process for incremental improvements that, in their aggregate, lead to cost savings or increased quality.
5. **Strategic Transfer**, a process of transferring technology or knowledge from one point to another for the purpose of leveraging capabilities.

The Originator-assisted system is featured in this book because it is the least understood or used, and has had the least written about it. Part of the reason the Originator-assisted system is overlooked is because it takes a lot of hard work, care, and patience. It also is the system that is most founded in the type of people principles discussed in this book as a whole. Although the rewards can be enormous, few have the disposition or the patience to separate the few good ideas from the large number that are generated. One executive told me, "Just give me the 'Good idea,' that's all I want. If you can't tell the good from the bad, just give me a list and I'll tell you!" That would be nice, but it doesn't work that way. The reason you can't tell the difference is because the process depends on a probability function. It is like opening a bag of popcorn kernels and predicting which ones will *not* pop.

The Office of Innovation at Kodak was set up to assist people with ideas that did not fit into the normal channels of their work and to allow the best ones to move forward. The philosophy behind an Originator-assisted system is simple. People are helped with developing and presenting their ideas and are given access to appropriate resources within the organization. Appropriate help continues until the concept is either dropped or developed sufficiently to carry through the normal company channels. This process involves people from all levels of the organization and all departments, and is a feeder mechanism to the larger organization. The process fulfills the needs of originators, while respecting company resources and producing successful innovations. Some terms are used in a special way for the Originator-assisted system. While a few definitions are found in the text, Appendix B contains a full glossary of innovation terms.

The difficulties, obstacles, inefficiencies, and time delays of an informal system are enormous. The greatest delay is the inability of an organization to commit to the correct concept. The system's function is to provide an opportunity feeder to the organization. Consider the story of Post-it™ Notes.[18] Post-it Notes did not just spring into existence one day, cheered on by upper management to the delight of the marketing department. The opposite was true. In 1962, 3M engineer Spencer Silver was trying to create a super-strong adhesive; instead, he created a super-weak one. Jim Fredrick, writing for the *Working Woman* magazine, described it this way. "He consulted his colleagues in glue at 3M. No one could think of a use for it. A glue that didn't stick very well

---

[18] Jim Frederick, "The End of Eureka!" *Working Woman*, February 1997, p. 38.

somehow seemed contrary to the whole point."[19] Silver still tried to promote the glue to marketing, but was rejected. Finally, he and the other engineers he had consulted dropped the idea all together.

Another engineer, Art Fry, had a different problem. He was using slips of paper as bookmarks and, much to his annoyance, they kept falling out of his books. He wondered if Silver's useless glue might come to his aid. He tried it and was delighted to have bookmarks that would stick to the page when he wanted them to and which didn't tear the page when removed. He tried to convince the marketing people at 3M that this new product was useful and might even make some money for the company. No one in marketing was interested in adhesive bookmarks. Fry was persistent. He pursued and pushed the idea until one day, five years later, he had a bright idea. He figured if anyone could find a use for these things and get the attention of decision-makers, the secretaries could do it. So, he passed out samples of the sticky bits of paper to the secretaries at 3M. In the words of Jim Fredrick, "The secretaries not only found a use for them, but they quickly became addicted. Fry's ad hoc production of samples soon began to fall behind the increasing demand, and finally, at the urging of their own secretaries, the top brass realized they could no longer ignore these 'press-and-peel notes,' as Post-its were then called. Sixteen years later, the Post-it Note is one of the five most popular products in the $15 billion company. It took five years to move from Spencer Silver's discovery to test marketing of the first commercial pad."[20]

Enterprising people innovate even when there is no formal system. Truly creative individuals are hard to stop. They can be stifled and curtailed, but they rarely give up. There have even been innovations in hostile environments, including

---

[19] Ibid.

[20] Ibid.

prison laborers in concentration camps. Transforming an idea within an organization into a quantifiable gain when there is no formal system is both difficult and unusual. The Originator-assisted system aids enterprising people by providing encouragement and removing many barriers thereby increasing the number of potentially useful ideas that come forward. It is uniquely designed to give unplanned ideas a home and an opportunity to be developed. Few managers appreciate either the value of, or difficulty in, finding good ideas. Even fewer managers realize that many potentially great ideas are buried within their own organizations. What is needed is a means to start them on a journey to fulfillment.

The Innovation Journey

> *Anything that the mind can conceive, and believe, can be achieved.*
>
> *—Napoleon Hill (1883-1970), motivational author.*

The innovation journey (see Appendix D) from concept to a quantifiable gain can appear to be short and sweet. More often it is long, tortuous, and stony. And when one step is taken, it is not always clear what the next step will be. Navigating the originator and the idea through the corporate developmental labyrinth is, in itself, an art form. The novelist, E.L. Doctorow could have been describing the innovation journey when he said, "It's like driving a car at night. You never see further than your headlights, but you can make the whole trip that way." Figure 3.1 shows the components of the idea connection process.

The three phases of this process—ideation, sifting, and securing a sponsor—are independent, interdependent, and essential. It is possible to generate ideas in multiple ways and to sift them in multiple ways, but if no sponsor is found, the potential of the idea will not be realized, regardless of its merits. Sifting includes several independent processes, which are defined below.

Phase I

1. **Idea Generation**. When someone generates an idea, that person is the originator and starts the process by connecting with the Originator-assisted system.

Phase II

2. **Enhancement**. This is a crucial part of the process and takes place early, between the innovation advocate and the idea originator. The advocate helps the originator view the idea from several perspectives with the intent of building upon its positive elements. At the same time, the idea's weaknesses are examined and there is consideration as to whether or not something already exists which would do what the originator wants to accomplish. This is the time when the pitfalls and obstacles of driving the idea through the organization are explored. It also gives the innovation advocate and the originator an opportunity to determine whether or not the originator has enough passion to face the problems associated with taking it further.
3. **Business Concept and Documentation**. During this stage, the innovation advocate works with the originator to transform the idea into sound business and technical concepts. The idea is written up and supporting documents are assembled.
4. **Peer Review**. Internal consultants (see Appendix B) are selected who can provide an initial screening for the idea. Actually, there may be several groups of people

assembled to examine the idea from different perspectives or at different phases of its development.

5. **Team**. A team of experts needs to be assembled to refine and move the idea forward. Prototypes may have to be built.

6. **Champions**. While working with the teams, one or more champions are sought who get excited about the idea, are able to allocate some corporate resources (e.g., time and possibly money) to the project, and do whatever is necessary to move the process along.

Phase III

7. **Sponsor Connection**. This is the final step for the advocate. It is when the team searches for and receives sponsorship (financial support) and a new advocate. The idea is then placed in an appropriate place within the ongoing stream of business development.

Figure 3.1: Originator-assisted System Generic Model

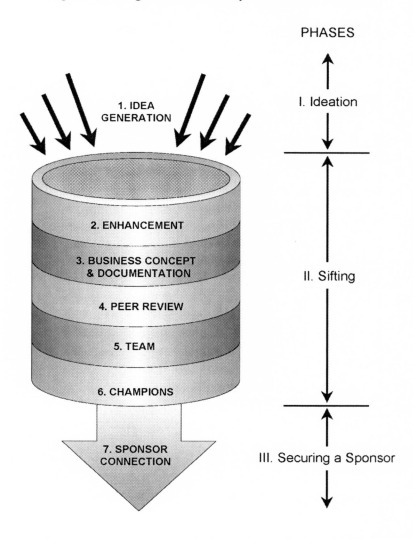

All ideas go through the same process in their journey from conceptualization to quantifiable gain. Regardless of the innovation systems used, ideas are generated, sifted, and a sponsor is secured.

George's Journey

The experience of George D'Ambrosia illustrates the Originator-assisted process. He had a high school diploma and an Associate of Applied Science degree, but was not an engineer. While in the service he had worked in wire communications. Later, at Kodak, he was a technician and senior product design drafter. He had a good reputation for his work, but was not among those the company looked to for new ideas.

In 1977 tragedy struck his life. George had a cousin, Frank Celento, who was his closest friend. They lived near each other, grew up together, and were closer than most brothers. In the early morning hours of September 10, an intruder entered Frank's home and both Frank and his wife, Loretta, were robbed and brutally murdered.

George was devastated. If they'd had an adequate security warning device, he thought they might still be alive. George became obsessed with security. He installed a security system in his own home and for several years he studied security systems and technology. All the systems he investigated had some basic weaknesses. He couldn't help but feel that something better could be developed, something that would have given Frank and Loretta adequate warning.

Between 1977 and 1985, George came up with an idea for residential security that used heat sensing and infrared technology coupled to a 35 mm photographic system. When he saw that the system could be easily defeated, he shelved that idea, hoping to come up with a better one.

In early 1985, he was at home watching the detective show "Kojak" on television. During a scene where a suspect was tracked, George thought of his cousin's tragic murder and had a flash of inspiration. Combining several technologies, he came up with the essence of a new concept within an hour and a half.

George knew he had a good idea and that it would work, but he didn't know what to do with it. He was not working on security, so he couldn't share it with his supervisor. He wasn't an engineer, so he didn't think anyone at work would take his idea seriously. In the past he had informally disclosed some ideas and other people took them and used them as their own. He was distrustful and stymied, so he just sat on his idea for several months.

Through a coworker, George heard the Office of Innovation helped people who had ideas, but he was suspicious. Would they listen to him? Would they take him seriously? He wondered. Maybe they would give his idea to someone else. Perhaps he could get into trouble with his supervisors for working on something outside the area of his responsibility.

After thinking about it for a few weeks, George realized that if he didn't find someone to share the idea with, it would never be developed and it would simply fade away. He decided to check out the Office of Innovation. He called me, and said he had an idea he wanted to talk about "off the record." He wanted to meet in a neutral place, outside of normal working hours. I agreed.

The meeting was held outside the company, after working hours, but George wasn't ready to share his best idea. He still didn't trust the system. Instead, he talked about the one he had already decided would be easy to defeat. His intent was to test the system to see what would happen. I listened carefully and encouraged George to proceed.

Then, I explained how the office worked and told George to mull it over. If he wanted to go ahead, he should call me. If he decided not to do anything more, that would be all right too. The idea would be kept confidential and it was up to George to decide whether or not to go ahead. George waited a few weeks to see if anything negative would happen. Nothing bad happened, so he decided to call me again. Only this time, he talked about his more recent and far-superior security concept. His innovation journey had begun.

Generation. The Office of Innovation at Kodak invited people to come in for an initial, candid, non-judgmental discussion with an innovation advocate about any ideas they may have.

Figure 3.2: Office of Innovation Eastman Kodak Company (1978-1988)

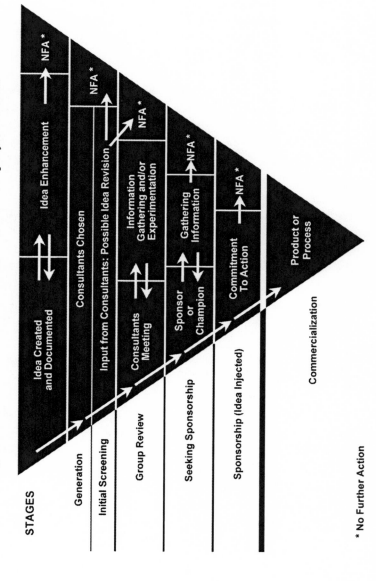

George was given an opportunity to talk about the idea.
We reviewed existing drawings and documents and
made it clear that he was responsible for pushing his
idea forward. We had a candid discussion on the
difficulty and the low probability of getting the idea
accepted. I let him know what to expect.

A major part of the early stages involves enhancement. Innovation advocates need to be carefully trained in this critical area. Assisting the originator with enhancement requires great sensitivity. Not everyone can do it. Suggestions are made, but mostly it is a time to help the originator see what is right about the idea and build on its strengths. It is also a time to look at the weaknesses and to explore whether or not something already exists that does what the originator wants to accomplish.

The originator needs to be counseled concerning the pitfalls and obstacles of driving this concept through the organization. This counseling serves two purposes: 1) to inform the originator about the process, and 2) to help the advocate determine whether or not the originator has enough passion to face the problems associated with driving the project through to completion.

Successful innovation is based on more than the value of the concept. Even the best idea does not go very far unless the person behind it is firmly convinced that it is good. That same person has to be willing to push hard to make the idea succeed. The more unusual the notion, the more passion is needed to push it through (see Chapter 4). Many people think they can generate ideas and let someone else develop them. That usually fails. Ideas are cheap; what's not cheap is the sweat to drive them! If the originator is not excited nor willing to invest enough energy, it is unlikely that anyone else will pick up on the idea.

In George's case, he had the needed drive and passion.
He did not have trust in the system or a workable network
of resources. He needed help to get the cooperation of the

right people. He was still fearful that since he was a product-design drafter rather than an engineer, his high-tech idea would not be taken seriously, or worse, that someone else would steal it or that the company might assign it to someone better equipped to see it through. With the assistance of the Office, George completed an Idea Memorandum, # 691, which described the device, its capability, and its core technology. The memorandum was refined and when completed, both George and I signed it before sending it to internal consultants.

The originator, in consultation with the advocate, selects internal consultants; the final choice, however, is made by the originator. Originators can have the material sent out anonymously if they wish.

George selected consultants who were technical people rather than those involved with finance, marketing, production, or other functions. I suggested some people from marketing who might be helpful and George agreed. He chose to have his name on the Idea Memorandum because he had selected consultants with whom he had worked, people who knew the quality of his work and his technical knowledge and skill.

Initial screening. Once the originator has decided to go ahead with the idea, the memorandum is signed and witnessed, then sent to the internal consultants along with a questionnaire.

After 80% of the questionnaires were returned, another meeting took place during which George and I reviewed the comments.

This is a delicate part of the procedure because sometimes comments are favorable and other times they are brutally negative. It is the task of the advocate to help the originator accept negative comments as objective input for consideration, rather than take the comments personally. Anxiety and frustration are often high, so reassurance and encouragement help the originator remain positive about the concept and submitting other ideas.

> *Most of George's reviews were positive. In fact, there was an air of excitement about them. A number of pertinent questions were raised and some good suggestions were offered. Based on the flavor of the positive replies, George decided to take the idea to the next stage.*

Group review. This involves a meeting of qualified experts. Once again, the originator has the final voice in selecting members of the group. Often, some of the original consultants are asked to serve again.

> *George decided to make the presentation to selected experts from within his own corporate division and research labs from other divisions. These experts were mainly engineers who were several grades higher than he on the organizational chart. He knew that if his work was to get anywhere it had to be endorsed by engineers who were respected in their fields.*

The group-review meeting is crucial. More than acceptance is at stake. This is the time to discuss possible refinements and find champions who can get excited about various aspects of the idea and push the concept forward. Having champions who will drive concepts forward until a sponsor can be found is key to success.

Before making this presentation, the originator makes a list of advantages and concerns generated by the reviews from the original screening consultants. This is done with the guidance of the advocate. Things are getting serious when the process reaches this point. All relevant aspects and implications of the idea are open for exploration. Factors needing more research are discussed and possible ways to continue the research are examined. Technical and challenging questions are raised to see how good the idea is, to look for risks, and to find fatal flaws. The group-review attendees are each sent the idea memorandum with all the comments of the original screening consultants and the list of concerns and advantages. This is sent out about two weeks before the meeting so there will be ample time to review the relevant documents.

Generally, there are multiple meetings. Participants bring new information and make plans for taking the idea further. The group review is often complicated. It frequently involves people from different departments, different cultures, and different mindsets, each with different objectives and different priorities. Because of the importance of this meeting, proper strategy is vital. The innovation advocate often consults with and coaches the originator beforehand on how best to proceed. Even such things as the appropriate way to dress are discussed. It is during this stage that obstacles, such as cultural differences among the various areas of the company (see Chapter 6), are overcome. The innovation advocate has the challenge of keeping the meeting focused on the potential of the idea and the best way to proceed.

George was lucky. Presenting his concept to his own corporate division minimized the cultural differences that often interfere with good communication and getting an idea accepted. But, he also had to present his idea to people he had not worked with, and others who were outside his area of responsibility because of its microelectronics core technology. George's background in microelectronics and layout design added to his credibility.

Seeking Sponsorship. Once the idea goes this far, it is necessary to find someone in the organization who has the authority to turn the concept into a project. This is a major step, involving a line-item allocation of company resources.

Finding a sponsor is the difference between an idea continuing or ending, so potential sponsors are under consideration from the outset. Again, the initiative and drive to push the idea along is up to the originator, who may be supported by champions. The innovation advocate assists in looking for sponsorship and helps the originator with the preparation of materials so the idea has the best possible chance for acceptance. The Office of Innovation also had access to technical people who could help with early experimentation, feasibility testing, and presentations.

When someone in the organization with responsibility for managing profit and loss sponsors the idea, the idea then becomes a project. This sponsorship includes a commitment to action on the part of the company. The idea then enters the normal channels of development and the primary function of the Office of Innovation is completed. Its role changes from being a major player to being available for consultation on an as-needed basis.

In George's case, there was more than one champion. Each played a key role at strategic times, but the first gate George had to get past was the group review. This produced a setback since the group decided that, although innovative, the idea did not fit the product base of Kodak's line of business. George had to find a new champion. That new champion was New Opportunity Development (NOD), which was designed to give limited assistance to ideas that were not part of Kodak's normal line of business, but had substantial business possibilities in areas that were related and into which business opportunities might grow. NOD also had the responsibility of launching new ventures outside of the realm of Kodak's non-standard lines of business. George was allocated $10,000 to conduct initial market research and prepare a summary business plan, development plan, and concept feasibility study. These disciplines were outside of George's training and *experience. The only thing that kept his panic at bay was his confidence that he understood the technology well enough to work out the concept-feasibility study. He enlisted a business and marketing consultant to help with research and writing the business plan. To his inexperienced surprise, $10,000 did not go very far, although he was able to get the services of an engineer and businessman to help write the business case. These consultants, interviewed by NOD and the advocate, were found to be qualified, so they proceeded.*

George and the consultants completed the requirements on time and within budget, and presented them to NOD. George made the technical presentation and the consultants presented those portions representing their areas of expertise. The presentation was well received and there were many questions. NOD realized that $10,000 would be insufficient. Based on the work done so far, and the excellent team that George had assembled, NOD decided to sponsor further exploration and George received another grant of $25,000.

A new challenge came with the grant. George was told to develop a more extensive business plan. Again, George found himself in a frightening and unfamiliar situation. He wasn't sure what an extensive business plan should look like or how much time he would need, but his passion for the project and his determination held strong. Within two weeks, working on his own time and with the assistance of the Office of Innovation, George wrote an outline of what was required to write a full business and marketing plan. In order to get all the necessary marketing information, George attended seminars and traveled a lot. He went from coast to coast seeking crucial knowledge of the security market while still attending to his regular work. At this point, NOD became the sponsor.

When the money from the second grant was exhausted, George and his small team made the final presentation to NOD. In spite of the positive comments by industry leaders and the excellent opportunity demonstrated by the technology, a decision was made not to fund the project any further because the development cost would be too high and the pay-back time too long. That meant that George lost his sponsor and he needed a new one for the concept to move on.

Kodak had scheduled a technology fair (Techfair) so that inventors within the company could display their new technologies, and build synergy and technical awareness within the company. Both NOD and the Office of Innovation were eager for George to display his concept at the Techfair and, hopefully, find a new sponsor. In order to qualify for the Techfair, George had to build a functional device that demonstrated the core technology. Up to this point, all he had were technical descriptions and some engineering software that modeled how the concept worked.

George and I consulted and he decided to go directly to the top echelons of his senior division management. This division employed more than 1,200 highly skilled technical people. If he could get support from his management, it would be a major step forward and he would be able to make a demonstration at the Techfair. That meant another presentation.

George was nervous; he knew this was a make or break situation. I helped him as he carefully prepared for the presentation. He divided the presentation with each member of the team presenting appropriate parts. Management was informed of the technical value and its potential as new, patentable technology. The catch was that a functional demonstration model had to be built in time for the Techfair. George explained that he needed an interim sponsor to help him find a full sponsor. The presentation was well received and George was instructed to make out a budget, complete with phases and gates, assemble a team of engineers and technicians, and build a functional concept model for the Techfair.

George's projected budget was $150,000, and it was based on a four-month schedule. The budget and timeline were approved by George's management, and the money was made available in stages. After successfully completing one stage, he would pass through that gate to receive money for the next. Throughout this time, team members still had to keep their commitments to other projects. George said they were the best team of dedicated individuals with whom he had ever worked. He was authorized to work on the project on company time. He could reduce his other duties, but not abandon them altogether. By this time, George's credibility was fully established and the concept was receiving serious attention. However, in order to conserve funds allocated for the project, George still did much of the work on his own time. His confidence and enthusiasm grew, buoyed by the support of the Office of Innovation, his management, work group, and others who had helped. He had the exhilarating experience of watching his idea grow and gain greater acceptance.

The demonstration model was completed for the Techfair on schedule and within budget. The presentation at the Techfair was a major success, the model performed flawlessly, and the concept was proven. It even caught the attention of Colby Chandler, Kodak's CEO. Chandler shared George's interest in security technology because of personal experience when his daughter's home had been burglarized.

Because of the Techfair, George found a sponsor, but the existing business and development plan was not sufficient. Once again, George found himself embarking on a new level of sophistication when he had to conduct better market research for strategic market positioning, and a more detailed financial and manufacturing plan. This experience, however, made George an expert in technology business planning. He became an eagerly sought internal consultant for making manufacturing, technological, and business plans that could show how well-thought-out concepts were worthy of development for new, high-tech products.

From the time of his cousin's murder, George had been studying security systems and traveling extensively in pursuit of a better understanding. He visited and consulted with security experts from major world security companies and government agencies from coast to coast. He gave presentations, held focus groups, and wrote reports for both commercial and government security seminars. All of this meant new experiences for George. For ten months, from November 1985 to September 1986, I worked with George and his concept intimately and intensely so he could find people in various departments that could assist him in this process and help present his ideas in the most favorable way.

Overall, about 20% of the ideas submitted to the Office of Innovation find a champion. About half of those (10%) make it to the point where they receive official sponsorship. George and his idea were among that exclusive and honored group of 10%.

Figure 3.3 illustrates the idea attrition curve over a number of years resulting in sponsored ideas.

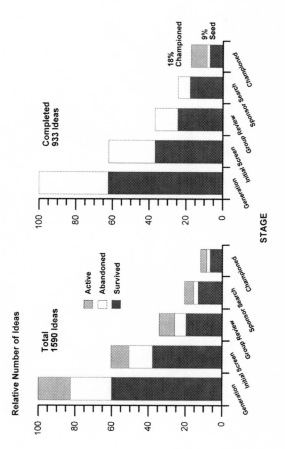

Figure 3.3: Idea Attrition Chart

At each stage of the innovation process, ideas can be classified as active (still under consideration), abandoned (no further action being taken), or survived (moved on to the next stage). The total number of ideas at each new stage is the same as those that survived from the previous stage. The chart on the right gives a snapshot of the processes' yield in time. It focuses on those ideas that were completed (either abandoned or survived), and disregards the ones still under consideration (active).

Understanding this decay curve is fundamental to understanding both the philosophy behind and the operation of an Originator-assisted system. Of every hundred ideas in the generation stage, about 60% of them go on to the next level. The originators decide to abandon the 40% that do not continue.

Out of the 60% that make it to the initial screening stage, about 66% of those make it to the next stage of group review. Originators abandon about half of those ideas. That leaves about 40% of the original 100 that go on to group review. There is further reduction and about 30% of the original completed ideas make it to a serious search for sponsorship. Not all of those ideas get adopted. Approximately 10% find sponsorship and, in the end, approximately 4% of the original 100 get adopted and are commercialized. Not all those ideas are commercially successful.

Looking carefully at the figures shows that nearly all that are abandoned are dropped when the originator realizes they will not go any further. The burden for showing value is up to the originator. He must prove that something will work rather than the company having to prove that it will not work. When the originator decides not to continue with a project, the innovation advocate plays a pivotal role in making sure there has been a positive experience. The originator is congratulated for taking the idea as far as it did go and there are discussions to identify the lessons learned from the experience. There is also encouragement for the originator to come back with other ideas. Most of them do. When people who had submitted ideas were surveyed, more than 90% of them indicated they would use the system again when they had another idea.

Effectiveness. How effective is an Originator-assisted system? There are three impressive measures: 1) commercial success, 2) benefits to the originator, and 3) additional benefits to the company.

Commercial Success.

After 2,500 ideas had been submitted to the Office of Innovation at Kodak, we found that 10% of the ideas made it to the sponsorship stage and 4% of the total were adopted. The figures are somewhat lower than actual outcomes because when the study was done, there were still ideas in the pipeline. Many of the pending ideas that were championed later received sponsorship.

While there were few successes from a percentage point of view, these successes reaped huge rewards. The 100 that made it to sponsorship (out of 2,500 submitted) produced $300 million in revenue (in 1987 dollars) from new ventures, products, and product extensions with a projection of $1.2 billion over the next five years. There was an additional $24 million in bottom line cost savings for the company. It cost the company less than $8 million to fund the Office of Innovation. The process can be compared to mining for gold. A lot of dirt and other minerals have to be removed before valuable nuggets are found. It pays to move a lot of debris to get the gold. The number or percent of successes is not important. What is important is the impact of those successes. That is why it is so important to get a large number of ideas and let the process take care of selection. This is an innovation prospecting technique that works. Figure 3.4 gives the distribution of adopted ideas.

Robert B. Rosenfeld

Figure 3.4: Distribution of Adopted Ideas

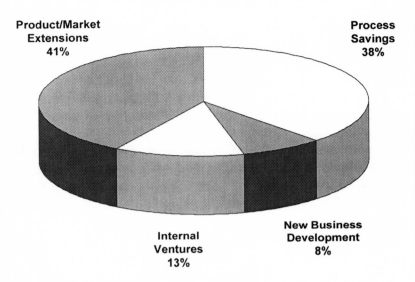

The pie chart shows the areas that were affected by the ideas that came through the Office of Innovation.

The value of the concepts that do not make it to completion should not be minimized. They are the reservoir of ideas out of which the really valuable ones come. The Office of Innovation kept records of ideas that were rejected. Many of them were revived when competitors came out with a similar product.

When people understand the low probability of success, they can more easily accept the fact that their ideas may not be adopted. Knowing this actually encourages them to come forward with more ideas. Sooner or later, they might have a winner, and it might be a big one.

> *In George's case, a business decision was made by Kodak not to develop the idea further because it dealt more with security than with imaging, and the company decided to concentrate on imaging technology. Although his idea was not among the 4% adopted, its value was recognized*

and George was encouraged to seek a market outside of Kodak. He sold the idea to a major defense contractor who put it into practical service in military applications. While George's device did not become a big moneymaker for either Kodak or George, both were compensated for their investment of time and money, and George received recognition and a promotion.

Success stories from the Office of Innovation are found in: Positive Turbulence by Gryskiewicz (1999), Corporate Creativity by Robinson and Stern (1997), When Giants Learn to Dance by Kanter (1989), and Readings in Innovation edited by Gryskiewicz and Hills (1992).

Benefits to the Originator

George found himself on a faster career-advancement track because of the experience he gained and the reputation he earned while working on this project. He received recognition and promotions on a level that would not have been possible had he followed a "normal" career path. His demonstrated persistence, and his technical and business competence led to assignments which he might not otherwise have received.

George's need to develop both an abbreviated and later a full business plan for a highly technical product resulted in his becoming an acknowledged expert in high-tech business planning. He was given a new position as an Electronics Products Business Planner. He has since participated in planning the development of Technological Business Plan Guidelines for new and emerging technologies.

On June 7, 1989, George was awarded the prestigious Heron of Alexandria Award for the invention of the Laser

*Radar Technology and his work with the United States
government in the interest of national security. This
award is given by the Quintillian Institute of George
Mason University and government securities agencies.
He was honored with a special recognition dinner in
Washington, D.C., which was attended by many
government security professionals.*

*As of this writing, George has retired from Kodak and
has started his own business.*

Additional Benefits to the Company

An Originator-assisted system can be the most effective
and economical training program available to a company. At
the Office of Innovation, we discovered that people worked
harder, more effectively, and more creatively on their normal
assignments when they were also working on a concept of
their own through the Office. Even though work on their idea
was being done on their own time, they were more productive
during company time. Lethargic employees often became
energized because of the new, additional challenge of working
on something special that was their own.

Employees embarking on the innovation journey
demonstrate and strengthen qualities of persistence, ingenuity,
and energy as they develop an uncommon degree of dedication
and diligence that becomes their work ethic and habit. At the
same time, working on new innovations gives highly
motivating exposure to new ideas and learning. In addition,
an extraordinary sense of loyalty to the company often
develops during this process. Highly critical employees become
tempered and even develop into corporate boosters.

In brief, employees who participate in innovation projects
are transformed. They become those "right people" who are
the greatest asset of any organization.

In George's example, he was able to provide the company with new levels of expertise and new areas of competence. George established networks in the security business and other areas of electronics, which were advantageous to Kodak in technical, business, marketing, and other situations.

*　　*　　*

Innovation Advocate

Effective innovation advocates are crucial for the success of an Originator-assisted system. There must be a sufficient number of dedicated advocates when an Originator-assisted system is set up to handle the flood of ideas. If there are not enough trained and competent advocates to deal with the ideas, those ideas cannot be processed in a timely manner. This causes frustration at all levels.

I was asked to set up an Originator-assisted system for a Fortune 500 company, but the operation was understaffed for budgetary reasons. They got more ideas than they could handle, and the system became known as the "black hole" because no one ever heard from people in the system again! The flood of ideas exceeded the company's capacity to deal with them. It is a great loss when an organization is not responsive to potential innovations outside its established channels. The prospective innovators may leave to work for someone else who appreciates their talents, or they may form new, competitive companies. Sometimes stifled workers invest their creative talents in interests outside the workplace that have nothing to do with the objectives of the organization. In some cases, they may continue to put in their time, but with reduced enthusiasm. By default, the company loses out on creative talent it didn't even know it had.

Not everyone can become an innovation advocate. To be successful one must be:

- **Centered on people and their ideas.** A genuine concern for people is a great stimulant and elicits many fresh ideas. It dissipates fear and suspicion while making people comfortable and eager to bring their ideas forward. Just looking for ideas, without regard for the people who have them, is seen as being self-serving and is not effective. An infectious enthusiasm for people and their ideas tends to stimulate creative thinking.
- **Sufficiently experienced and competent technically to understand what the originator hopes to achieve.** People come to the Originator-assisted system with concepts that are only partially thought through. Advocates help structure these notions into business terms, or direct the originator to people who can assist in this essential step.
- **Results oriented.** Knowing what it takes to get a job done, then taking appropriate action is key to success.
- **Respected and trusted by coworkers throughout the organization.** When there is no respect and trust, people will not use advocates. They will be seen as "political appointments."
- **Politically astute.** Advocates need to be politically savvy and know what is going on throughout the organization, but not use their skill and knowledge for personal advantage. Advocates lose their credibility when they are seen as being involved with political manipulation for their own interests.
- **Aware of why and how an idea fails.** They must be sensitive to the dynamics of the innovation process and be able to communicate successes, failures, and partial successes in ways that encourage the generation of more ideas. They also need to convey to originators that they understand what it takes to push the idea forward and that they can help.
- **Skilled at networking.** The innovation advocate needs a broad network within the organization to secure the

assistance of others, such as those skilled in business concept development or marketing. This means interfacing with many different people from different departments and divisions representing the full spectrum of cultures, priorities, mind-sets, and perspectives that exist within the organization. This takes superb people skills and a high level of diplomacy.

- **Detached**. Advocates need to be detached and objective. While they need to be astute and honest in appraising the value of an idea, they should always be mindful that the success of an idea cannot be predicted in the beginning. Those who claim they can tell are parading arrogance. The accuracy of their predictions is generally no better than fifty-fifty. There are a few rare individuals who have an uncanny knack for picking winners. It is interesting that although they tend to justify their choices analytically, in fact, the process they rely on tends to be intuitive.

Managing a System

Even though innovation is everyone's business, not everyone has a talent for idea generation. Twenty percent of the people who submit ideas are responsible for 80% of the ideas generated. They are "preferred customers" and should be treated that way.

In order for innovation to flourish and be sustained, both the spirit and the form need to be vigorous. An innovation leader creates an environment in which the animating spirit of innovation can produce results.

But, no structure alone produces that animating spirit. It is the passion that comes from deep within the originator. Without passion and persistence, even the best of ideas will not go forward, and with passion comes pain, the hidden ingredient.

CHAPTER 4

Passion Is The Fuel And Pain Is
The Hidden Ingredient

One of the things you get from the literature of the saints is the dark night of the soul, the raging of the passions. Men are driven to greatness by these raging passions. If you're too much in control, you're not free to take life's toughest challenges.

—Andrew Young (1932-), U.S. Ambassador to the United Nations (1977-79).

Ideas do not propel themselves; passion makes them go. Passion is the fuel that generates an intense desire to move forward, smashing through barriers and pushing through to conclusions. This chapter examines the nature of passion, the people with passion, and pain, the hidden ingredient in any important enterprise. It provides suggestions for managing both the passion, and the pain.

As an eager and energetic young research chemist working at Eastman Kodak Company, I had a lot of wild ideas. Fortunately, my laboratory head, Bob

Bacon, saw my spirit and helped me focus it constructively. While I had spirit, I was also highly critical of the company and its policies, but this did not bother Bacon. Instead of trying to keep me in line, he challenged me with problems. He would say, "You have the skills; do you want to see if you can make this work?"

I would say, "Sure." Then, I'd spell out certain conditions. The impetuous demands did not bother Bacon. He saw a passion for tackling work and solving problems, and overlooked the haughtiness by simply saying, "Okay, let's talk and work it out."

With that, I would throw myself into projects. Bacon became a mentor and continued to work with me by keeping my energies focused on positive things inside the company. There were many stumbling blocks along the way, but I realized something interesting. Obstacles actually excited me and made me work harder. When passion met obstacles it actually served as a catalyst that generated even more creative energy. Then, I wondered about other people and discovered that the most productive ones were those who were the most excited and passionate about what they were doing.

With a burning intensity, passionate workers throw themselves into their work; the passion becomes a source of energy without which they cannot live. When they come up against a brick wall or a locked door, they say, "I'm going to break it down. I'm going to do whatever it takes to make this thing work. No one is going to stand in my way; nothing is going to stop me. I will pursue this with or without you." Passion, in addition to talent and skill, is really a valuable company asset. It struck me as odd that it had nothing to do with those things listed as assets. While there is no question about the importance of a positive balance sheet, or physical plants and equipment, the real assets of any company include people who get excited about what they are doing. It's a paradox: passion is what transforms other resources into profits, but it never shows up on a balance sheet.

Instead of being valued, passion scares many managers because they do not understand it, cannot control its intensity, and cannot see where it is heading. Those with passion are often seen as disruptive, arrogant and rebellious, and many of them are. It is threatening. Managers know that passion can disturb their whole department, generate unpredictable events, and upset the comfortable. And passionate people have been known to be wrong, sometimes disastrously wrong, making cautious managers wary.

Bureaucratic managers want to get rid of the problems associated with passion because it involves "sensitive" management that they want to avoid. So, in trying to stop the passion, life may become easier, but creative energy under such conditions may evaporate. Without creative energy, organizations can be thrown into downward spirals.

It takes someone like Bob Bacon to make passion work within an organization; someone who can serve as a mentor, who can protect both the person from the organization and the organization from the person.

The Nature of Passion

Nothing ever built arose to touch the skies unless some man dreamed that it should, some man believed that it could, and some man willed that it must.

—Charles F. Kettering (1876-1958), founder and head of research for General Motors, and innovation leader.

Passion has many facets. It is more than being highly motivated or wanting something intensely. It is being so obsessed with wanting to accomplish something or solving a problem that the individual forges ahead despite formidable obstacles. Following are some of its outstanding features.

Energy and Tenacity

One of the most prominent facets of passion is that it energizes those who have it and enables them to stick with projects. Consider the case of Thomas Edison (1847-1931) and the incandescent light. Edison did not invent the light bulb, but he invested the energy and persistence needed to make it practical.

Many people had found ways to use electricity to produce light, but the filaments burned out too quickly to be useful— that is, until the energetic, tenacious, and persistent Thomas Edison found a solution. In the words of his biographer, Thomas Boyd, "For eighteen to twenty hours a day he experimented with all sorts of materials, from human hair to plant fiber from the South Seas, until one day he found that carbonized bamboo fiber gave the best results. Most people would have stopped there, but not Edison. He had to find the best type of fiber. He had men search the forests of Cuba, Jamaica, Ceylon, and Burma for vegetable fiber and grass. He tested more than 6,000 such materials, and his investigations on this one thing alone cost a small fortune."[21] That means at least 5,999 unacceptable attempts.

Confidence

Another facet of passion is the confidence it instills. People who have it don't just think something can be done: they **know** it can be done!

One of the best examples of this is Charles Goodyear (1800-1860). For 10 years, Goodyear had been in and out of prison because he could not pay his debts.[22] His family was in want,

---

[21]   Thomas A. Edison Boyd, *Prophet of Progress*, E.P. Dutton and Co., New York. 1961, p. 114.

[22]   Nathan Goodyear Aaseng, *The Inventors*, Lerner Publications, Minneapolis, 1988, p. 7.

yet he pursued his dream of making rubber a workable product. Millions of dollars had gone into rubber research with no satisfactory results. The problem was that rubber got hard and brittle when cold, and soft, gooey, and smelly when hot.

Goodyear was sick, malnourished, and poverty stricken when his friend William DeForest visited him. DeForest found him living in a third-floor walk-up studio apartment crammed with gum and chemicals. As he entered his cluttered room, Goodyear proudly exclaimed, "Here is something that will pay all my debts and make us comfortable." DeForest was unimpressed. He had been trying to help his friend, and now he was attempting to have him face reality. There was no future in rubber. The India rubber business was vanishing. Goodyear responded to this well-intended advice by pulling a piece of white rubber from his pocket, saying, "And, I am the man to bring it back again!" This supreme optimism, exhibited while Goodyear was surrounded by the debris of false starts and failures, eventually led to the discovery that saved the rubber industry. Later, in 1844, he obtained the patent for the vulcanization process that would revolutionize and dominate the rubber industry.

When President John F. Kennedy (1917-1963) announced the goal of putting a man on the moon within ten years[23], it seemed little more than a science-fiction dream. Nevertheless, bright, talented people were assembled who had the unshakable confidence and passion not just that it could be done, but that that it would be done. Six months ahead of schedule, Neil Armstrong stepped on the moon and announced that he had taken a "giant step for mankind."

Whether working alone like Goodyear, or in an institutional setting like the lunar project, passion with supreme confidence is a basic requirement for successful innovation.

---

[23]   Op. cit., Von Braun and Ordway, "Apollo Program," *Encyclopedia Americana*, 2000, vol. 25, pp. 381-383.

Resilience

Passion prevents setbacks from defeating the process. When you have passion, you are like a fighter who gets knocked down and gets up from the mat ready to go again. In fact, when the passion is strong, it is hard not to rebound from a setback.

The name Nobel is world renowned and associated with marvelous advances for humankind. Nathan Aaseng wrote that Alfred Nobel performed dangerous experiments. In fact, in 1864 Nobel had an accident with the unstable substance, nitroglycerin, which shattered the Nobel laboratory in Stockholm and killed several people, including Nobel's youngest brother. Frightened officials banned all experiments with nitroglycerin within the city, and Nobel was forced to carry out his work on a barge in the middle of a lake outside the city limits.[24] How many people would have continued on? It takes an extra measure of resilience to bounce back after such a tragic incident.

Challenge and Focus

For people of passion, a challenge is like the starting gun for a race: "Bang!" and away they go toward their clear objective. George Washington Carver (1864-1943) responded to a challenge in a systematic and energetic manner.[25] He knew that cotton was the most important cash crop for many southern farmers and he also knew that it robbed the soil of nitrogen. Legumes, such as peanuts, replenished the nitrogen that cotton needed, but had little commercial value. Carver was aware that cotton farmers did not want to waste their time, energy, and land on a crop that would not produce cash; they were focused instead on an immediate monetary return and their bottom line. Crop rotation was a strategy with which they did not want to bother.

---

[24] See Michael Evolanoff and Marjorie Beckman, *Alfred Nobel, the Loneliest Millionaire*, W. Ritchie Press, Los Angeles, 1969.

[25] See Gene Adain, *George Washington Carver*, Chelsea House, New York, 1989.

Carver thought that if there were some way that peanuts could be made profitable, farmers would rotate their crops, fortify their land, and make money doing it. While others might have realized such a situation, only Carver accepted the challenge to do something about it. "He experimented with peanuts and made over three hundred products including shampoo, shaving cream, paint, cooking oil, soap and even a kind of rubber."[26] Because Carver responded to a challenge, peanuts went from having little commercial value to being the sixth largest commercial crop in the United States.

Learning from Criticism

There is something about devoting energy to new and audacious projects that tends to generate a lot of criticism. People of passion, however, are so driven that they hardly notice criticism.

The Italian inventor Guglielmo Marconi (1874-1937) got criticism from every side. Today, he is best known as the inventor of the first practical radio-signaling system. His father "constantly harassed him as a good-for-nothing freeloader . . . [and his] formal schooling ended when he failed the entrance examination for the University of Bologna."[27] Despite the animosity of his father and the denial of further education, he plugged away until he figured out how to send radio signals over distance with a directional antenna. Before the end of the 19th century, Marconi was successful in sending a radio signal across the English Channel. In 1901, he communicated across the Atlantic Ocean. Toward the end of his life, Marconi was also testing shortwaves and microwaves. In brief, this "good-for-nothing freeloader," who had failed the entrance examination for higher education, contributed much to the development of radio and, in 1909, won a Nobel Prize.

---

[26]   Ibid., p. 104.

[27]   Nathan Aaseng, *The Inventors. Nobel Prizes in Chemistry, Physics, and Medicine,* Lerner Publications Co., Minneapolis, Minnesota, 1988.

People of Passion

> There is a small steam engine in his brain which
> not only sets the cerebral mass in motion, but keeps
> the owner in hot water.
>
> —*New York Weekly Mirror (July 5, 1845),*
> *referring to author Edgar Allan Poe.*

Extreme characteristics are a part of people who are passionately looking for a solution to a problem. These people are often seen as crazed and out of control, and many of them are. They are sometimes seen as aloof and withdrawn, and many of them are. Their peculiarities usually make them different from others within their organization so they are often seen as a threat.

People of passion seem oblivious to the kinds of punishments that send others scampering for cover, and traditional rewards are often meaningless. For them, the thrill of discovery is its own best reward. This is an internal event with which no one can tamper. Acceptance and approval by peers and superiors is less important to them than it is to most others. Money alone holds little motivation. The man who delivered flowers to Albert Einstein noticed, among other idiosyncrasies, that Einstein would use uncashed checks as bookmarks.[28] Time and social commitments are also secondary. Those who spend time with impassioned people learn that the phrase "just a minute" needs to be measured in geological time.

A man I once worked with had a perplexing challenge. He had to figure out the rate and nature of the flow of liquid from a huge tank, but the outlet was at the bottom. The tank was the size of a large room and he had only a few hours to get the information. There was no convenient way to do it. Right there in the workplace, he took off all his clothes, dove

---

[28] The florist is an old friend of John Kolstoe's. He related this story to John.

into the tank, swam to the bottom, took the measurements, and returned to his desk to make his calculations.

In no time at all, his telephone rang with a call from his supervisor. There had been complaints that someone was swimming naked in the tank and he wanted to know what was going on. Did he solve the problem? Yes. Did he solve it in a timely way? Yes. Was he completely disruptive? No question about it. Was he right? Right on target. Only an intense desire to get results could push someone to create such a spectacle in the workplace. Some managers would have fired him on the spot. Fortunately for him and his company, his supervisor was an innovation leader who applauded his passion and ingenuity for getting the needed information. His supervisor went back to the people who had complained, performed damage control, and calmed them down.

When the king asked Archimedes (287-212 B.C.) to determine if the crown he had was of pure gold, Archimedes was stumped because he knew of no way to get accurate measurements to compare weight to mass. Then, when he sat in his bathtub and watched the water rise, he reasoned that his body mass had displaced the water, causing it to rise. He leaped out of the tub, running naked through the streets shouting, "Eureka!" (I have found it!). Archimedes was a prolific contributor to science. Yet, he is best known for the displacement theory, not because it was more important than the others, but because of his nakedness. Today, he might be arrested for indecent exposure and sent for psychiatric evaluation. In an attempt to make him "sane," the world might be deprived of future discoveries.

Living with Passion

It is natural to want the brilliant results without the erratic behavior. We may tolerate some erratic behavior as long as it produces worthwhile results, but it is more complicated than that. To benefit from the good, it is necessary to expect and tolerate the bad. The innovation leader understands that you either accept people with passion, realizing there will be a generous supply of both successes and failures, or miss the extraordinary results that they, and they alone, produce.

The formation of a pearl is a good illustration of how an organism's response to an irritant is more important than the irritant. When a grain of sand finds its way into an oyster, the oyster starts to coat it with a special substance to render it harmless. The action of coating the grain of sand transforms it into a work of beauty. In my company, Idea Connections, we use the formation of a pearl to illustrate how an irritant can be transformed into the beauty of success. Within an organization, people of passion are irritants. They can either be expelled to make life easier, or they can be permitted to work their magic of forming pearls of success.

In general, managers have different tolerances for passion depending on their level of responsibility. There is a fair tolerance for passion at the lower end of the corporate hierarchy, but the higher a manager rises in the organization, the greater becomes his concern with conserving resources. Conformity becomes increasingly prized and the chaos of passion dreaded, because it consumes resources unpredictably.

Toward the top of the organizational chart, we have found that the value of passion is better understood. It is viewed as a highly desirable, if not essential, characteristic for driving extraordinary projects forward.

Ideally, tolerance for passion and its chaotic nature would be found at all levels of an organization. We have found that there is a good balance when approximately 10% of the work force consists of people with extraordinary passion.

Pain—The Hidden Ingredient

One of the greatest pains to human nature is the pain of a new idea.

—*Walter Bagehot (1826-1877), British economist.*

There seems to be some universal law that says when pursuing a passion or following a dream, pain is part of the process. A model from physical chemistry helps explain how pain works in the innovation process. Two or more compounds, called reactants, can interact to form a different and more stable compound. These compounds require energy to go from their original, separate and less stable state to their combined, stable condition. The energy required to do this is called the energy of activation. A catalyst can be used to lower the amount of energy required for the whole reaction. This is shown in Figure 4.1.

Figure 4.1: Energy of Activation (Hill of Pain)

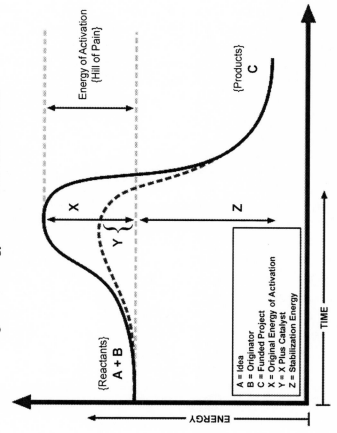

In the above diagram, A and B represent the reactants and C the resulting new compound. The energy required to activate the process without the catalyst is shown by X. The reduced energy needed when a catalyst is present is shown by Y.

This serves as an analogy for the innovation process. Let A represent an idea and B, the originator. When the idea is new, A and B's position is not secure. It takes energy, in the form of passion, just to get people's attention. C represents the point at which the idea is funded—the desired, more stable condition. Once attained, less energy is required to move forward. The greatest obstacles are usually in going from A/B to C. It is like going over a hill. There is also a lot of pain with this process, which is why I refer to it as the "hill of pain."

In the diagram, the amount of extra pain required to surmount the obstacles and get to the more stable (funded) state is represented by X. Once the needed energy has been exerted and the pain endured, it is possible to attain the preferred condition of C.

This process is repeated and a new "hill of pain" is encountered periodically from the inception of the idea to a quantifiable gain. With each successive occurrence, however, the energy needed to overcome obstacles is decreased until the project gets launched. Once the project has been funded it gains momentum, and less and less passion is needed to keep it moving. A point is reached where it actually takes more energy to stop a project than to keep it going.

At the early stages, when the "hill of pain" is high, the innovation leader plays a special role. She is the catalyst lowering the "hill of pain," or Y, thereby making it easier for A/B to get funding. Much of the counsel and assistance the innovation leader gives to the originator serves this function.

When passion is strong, pain does not matter as much and there is a willingness to sacrifice and endure tremendous pain. In fact, the derivation of the word "passion" comes from the Latin word, passion, which means physical suffering.

Athletes have been known to concentrate so hard on accomplishing their goals that they are unaware of pain. The body cooperates by producing endorphins that mask the pain, giving even greater tolerance and extending the limits of endurance. After an event, these athletes may collapse in exhaustion. Only then is attention given to the torment their body went through as they start to feel the pain. Ask any football player what he feels like the day after a game, but when recalling the event in the distant future, his talk will focus on the performance and his eyes will glow with reminiscence. Ask him about the agony, and he may well shrug and remind you that, "No pain, no gain!" One professional football player who had sustained severe injuries and pain said he welcomed the pain because he played better when there was pain.

When motivation is high, the burden of pain loses its power to deter. Recently, the medical records for President John F. Kennedy were available for review. From his youth on, he could have qualified under the current standard for Americans with Disabilities. His pain was constant. Yet, he carried on and gave no evidence that the excruciating and constant pain he endured interfered with his judgment or functioning as President.

There are many other examples of continuing on in spite of intense pain during emergency situations. Small women have been known to lift objects many times their own weight to free a child, pinned under a load—something they could never do under normal circumstances.

Both innovation leaders and entrepreneurs know pain. It is part of the dues paid for success. Successful executives and entrepreneurs all have amazing "war stories." They don't talk about them often, but they are never forgotten. Once they get started telling their stories, they talk about the long hours, going without food or sleep, waking up at 3 a.m. in a cold sweat, fear of failure, holding off creditors, and being desperately short of resources. They might also talk about the pain and indignities their families have had to suffer. All, without exception, have experienced a great deal of pain in launching their enterprises, although the difficult times are rarely talked about.

Who feels the pain?

Pain comes from many sources. Sometimes there is great anguish and frustration in trying to figure out the nature of a problem and attempting various solutions that don't always work. There may be many long days and sleepless nights. There may be rejection and ridicule with ideas ripped apart by friends, colleagues, and supervisors. Often, a person is so preoccupied by a problem that other important life matters are taken care of in a haphazard manner. This creates additional problems and pain: bills go unpaid, appointments are missed, and deadlines ignored. These lapses tend to increase the criticism from family and friends. Coworkers may become jealous or threatened by the work being done, or may find their workload increases because of the preoccupation and inattention of the one who is passionately pursuing some project. For whatever reason, there may be several individuals who will sabotage or even try to stop the project. Estrangement and divorce are common. Friends and family members feel the pain as the person in pursuit of a goal concentrates so hard on the project at hand that she becomes physically or emotionally separated from those close to her. When a person is seen to be "going overboard" with a project that causes disruptions for the department and pain for the manager. If the project does not have a direct bearing on the manager's primary objectives, it may even be viewed as insubordination.

Pain can also be created for coworkers either because they are suffering alongside the one in hot pursuit of an objective, or they are reacting against the intense passion. The passionate one may be neglectful of his regular duties, placing additional burdens on coworkers.

I know a story about a woman whose family was desperately poor while her father was pursuing an idea about which he felt strongly. It was winter and there was no money for fuel. She had some wooden building blocks that were thrown into the fire for heat. Even though she was an adult when telling the story, she said she could still see her mother throw her beloved toys into the fire because there was nothing else to burn.

Managing the Passion and the Pain

Passion cannot be forced on someone else. It is a precious, internal gift, and an asset that needs to be treated with care and appreciation. Innovation leaders need the ability to identify people who have passion for what they are doing and, at the same time, protect both those who have the passion and others around them.

The best innovation leaders capitalize on the sparks of passion within their people, keep them engaged in productive and meaningful activity, and thus generate even more innovations. Otherwise, people of passion will look elsewhere for a place to invest their energy.

Many senior executives understand this; they instinctively know how to drive an opportunity to completion. More frequently, problems lie with middle management and the executives who fear passion because they cannot control it.

Manage the passion, not the person

Managing the passion and not the person is subtle and involves giving an individual's passion the room it needs. It also involves keeping focused and making sure that the passion is not killed by mismanagement, nor that it damages the person or the organization.

A friend of mine was offered early retirement. It was such a good deal that it was almost impossible not to take it. Bill took the package and attended the retirement party, receiving all sorts of accolades for the good research he had done over the years. That was a Friday event. On Monday morning, Bill was back in the research labs continuing his research, his life's passion.

He saw no reason why being retired should interfere with the work he was doing. He viewed the retirement package as a quirk of paperwork that just changed the way he got paid and had nothing to do with his work. Fortunately, there was someone with authority who made arrangements that made it possible for Bill to keep on working. Bill wanted nothing more than the ability to pursue his passion, which was continuing his research, so why not come to work? A manager can see this either as a big headache or an opportunity in which both the individual and the organization will benefit.

Passion is not available on command

Bureaucratic managers, who see their organization as a fixed structure instead of a living organism, fall into the trap of thinking of people as replaceable parts. Those who know the value, but not the nature of passion, sometimes believe that they can simply assign a project and the passion will follow. It doesn't work that way. There has to be a special chemistry between the idea, or project, and the person. No matter where an idea originates, if someone can get excited about the idea and has the capacity to develop it, that person owns it. The innovation leader knows he or she cannot create the spark, but once found, it must be nurtured carefully.

Protect the one with passion

When people are excited about what they are doing, they create many dangers. Their excitement is such that a person may drive himself so hard as to lose perspective about other things. Part of the job of an innovation leader is to protect the people who are strongly passionate about an idea, both from others and from themselves. This is done by:

- *Interceding when necessary.* Some people within the organization will feel threatened by the person with passion. They can become formidable adversaries. The innovation leader needs to be alert to this danger and head off problems. One way to do this is to keep potential adversaries from learning too much about the project until it is well under way. At the same time, it is important to inform those who need to know what is going on. When possible, it helps to make allies of those who could be potential antagonists, or become a buffer and allay the fears of those who might otherwise attack. This takes time and sacrifice on the part of the innovation leader, but the objective of letting the one pursuing his ideas proceed with the least interference is well worth it.

- *Maintaining focus and sense of direction.* People with passion may become excited about many things at once; in some cases, it may be necessary to gently focus their attention so that their energy is not dissipated. If this is not done, they may spread themselves too thin, accomplish little, and hurt both themselves and others.

- *Providing encouragement.* Mismanagement kills passion and thwarts innovation. People capable of passion are often put down as "nerds," "odd-balls," or "crack-pots." People get kicked, and sometimes kicked hard, for having ideas that are different. Few are found to cheer them on, so they stop sharing their creative ideas. The ideas they do have are kept to themselves or focused in an entirely different direction. The innovation leader, without fawning, needs to be a cheerleader and give appropriate boosts of realistic support.

- *Finding a place in the organization where passionate people can fit.* Since people who are passionate are not always easy to get along with, and tend to drive others to distraction, it is often necessary for the innovation leader to become involved. If the person really seems to have both passion and capabilities, it is worthwhile for the innovation leader to take extreme measures to find some place where there can be a "fit." Charles Kettering was founder and head of research at General Motors. His biographer, T.A. Boyd,[29] described him as being especially clever about out-of-the-ordinary talents and keeping them within the organization when he saw that the value to the company was greater than the chaos caused by eccentricities.

---

[29]   Thomas Alvin Boyd, *Professional Amateur: The Biography of Charles Franklin Kettering,* Arno Press, New York, 1972.

A good innovation leader will look for those who are feeling pain, empathize with them, and help them work through it. Several proven techniques such as active listening, coaching, and analyzing what went right and what went wrong during the innovation process have been helpful.

It is also helpful to suggest a new project when pain becomes overwhelming. Sometimes, backing away from an endeavor and pursuing something different helps a person go back to the original project with a fresh perspective and renewed energy.

When frustration and anger manifest themselves and are allowed to fester, these emotions will undermine production. The innovation leader should allow the employee to express anger and frustration, without judging or trying to "explain away" the source of irritation.

Using humor in a sensitive way helps regain a sense of balance and composure and can be therapeutic. Often, when people are stuck on a particularly difficult or painful part of a project, relief through humor enables them to pursue the project with a fresh view and renewed vigor. Humor can be the most effective tool for healing, when it is used carefully and comes naturally. When forced or unnatural, it often backfires.

Generally, a small number of people come up with a majority of the ideas within an organization. Some of these ideas work out, most do not. When an idea does not work out, saying so does not always convince the originator she should stop. It is helpful to suggest that she pursue some of her other ideas, or offer something else to work on that might kindle the fire of passion. Unless the energy is redirected, there is a risk that she will hammer away on the idea, consuming time, energy, and other resources with increasing frustration.

All of the facets of passion—confidence, energy, tenacity, resilience, focus, challenge, disregard of criticism—require a trusting and intimate relationship between the innovation leader and the person with passion. In most cases, such relationships do not follow a traditional hierarchical structure.

People driven by passion generally do not have much respect for authority figures; they do however, respect competency and understanding. Both antagonists and allies are found throughout the organization. Antagonists are plentiful; allies are few and treasured. In the heat of battle, it is sometimes difficult to tell one from the other. It is the task of the innovation leader to guide, help distinguish the ally from the antagonist, and coach innovators on how to get support from the allies and diffuse the antagonists.

Obviously, encouraging passion doesn't mean that every idea that comes along is worthy of funding. Whether or not to fund something remains a business decision. A major factor in deciding if a project should be funded is the amount of passion the originator has for the problem or idea: the more unusual the project, the more passion it will take to push it through. The more difficult the task, the greater the passion needed to make it work. If the idea looks good, but there is no passion behind it, it will not develop into anything useful unless someone can be found to get fired up about it. Venture capitalists base 60% of their decision to fund a venture on the management team's commitment and passion for the enterprise.

The decision to stop funding an idea needs to be communicated with great tact. When it is seen that something is not going to work, the originator must be helped to understand this and have his energy redirected without killing enthusiasm. Celebrate with the person and compliment him for taking the idea as far as it has gone. Explain as clearly as possible why a business decision had to be made to discontinue the project, and at the same time let him know that you are genuinely eager to learn about his next idea.

Having looked at passion, it is time to consider the situation when two or more people have passion for an idea, and work well together. There are important times when it is necessary for them to be together physically, what I call co-locating.

CHAPTER 5

Co-Locate For Effective Exchange

The other reason the thing held together back then . . . we would get our managers together once a week and critique ourselves . . . And it worked so well . . . it just became part of our culture

—Sam Walton (1918-1992), founder of Wal-Mart stores.

In the business world, we use the term co-location to refer to physical proximity between people. It is a key for building the trust that is essential to the innovation process. It is also the best means to exchange information, get a cross-fertilization of ideas, stimulate creative thinking in one another, and critique ideas during their formative stage.

Why do companies spend billions of dollars every year transporting people all over the world for business meetings? Because it works. Co-location is the most effective way to communicate. Professional associations, trade groups, and conferences exist because it pays to have people get together. Even off-hand comments made during moments of relaxation have been known to change the whole character of a venture. Voice intonation and visual cues, which tell us more than words, are communicated by close proximity. Co-location is an opportunity to assess each other's strengths and weaknesses.

There are subtle and unknown elements of communication exchanged when people are physically together. McCraty, Atkinson, Tomasino, and Tiller[30] reported at the Fifth Appalachian Conference on Neurobehavioral Dynamics (1996) that cardiac signals from one person were picked up by electrodes on another person who was separated from the first person by 18 inches. Recent studies have highlighted the importance of pheromones—animal odors that affect the behavior of other members of the same species. The expression "something doesn't smell right" may have a basis in fact.

Women who live together tend to develop similar menstrual cycles.[31] Men who live together also tend to develop traits that are similar. The writer James Michener would spend months in areas he was writing about to get a sense of the place. Only after getting a feeling for the location would he start taking serious notes. One highly successful businessman was emphasizing the need for personal contact when he said, "I only do business with eyeballs." He was also expressing the power of the eyes, which have been called the windows to the soul.

It is not clear why proximity is so important. What is clear is that co-location affects people physically, emotionally, and mentally. Trust and confidence between people are enhanced

---

[30]   Rollin McCraty, Mike Atkinson, Dana Tomasino, and William Tiller, "The Electricity of Touch: Detection and Measurement of Cardiac Energy Exchange between People," *Proceedings of the Fifth Appalachian Conference on Neurobehavioral Dynamics: Brain and Values,* Lawrence Erlbaum Associates, Inc., Mahwah, New Jersey, 1997, p. 8.

[31]   See K. Stern and M.K. McClintock, "Regulation of Ovulation by Human Pheromones," *Nature* 1998, vol. 392, pp. 177-179.

when all the human senses are involved. What do people do when they really want to confide in one another? Even if they are all alone in a closed room, they tend to get physically close, usually eye-to-eye, and lower their voices even when there is no possible way anyone else can hear their conversation.

Many business conversations on the telephone end with, "We need to get together so we can discuss this face-to-face." Usually nothing is said at the physical meeting that couldn't have been said on the telephone, but the communication is different. In person the two people "scan" each other. Using all their senses, they evaluate sincerity, uncertainties, commitment, and trust issues.

Co-location may even entail the rearrangement of furniture. Two men I know started a successful venture. Both men had to travel a great deal and communicated as best they could through e-mail and the telephone, but when they were in the office at the same time, they had their desks together so they could face one another and share ideas immediately and easily. It was an effective way for them to launch their enterprise. They told me later that they could not have made the venture work if it were not for frequent, face-to-face discussions.

John Patterson (1844-1922), the effective, if unorthodox, founder of the National Cash Register Company, knew that the best way to understand what was going on in his company was to be on the spot. In 1894, a customer returned a large shipment of defective cash registers. Patterson was shocked to learn that they had been sabotaged by his own employees, who had poured acid into the mechanisms. Having previously devoted his attention to sales and marketing, he quickly moved his desk onto the factory floor to find the cause. He discovered that his employees "had no heart in their jobs; they did not care whether they turned out good or bad work. Then (he) looked further into conditions and (he) frankly had to confess to (himself) that there was no particular reason why they should put their heart into their work."[32]

---

[32]   See A.G. Robinson and S. Stern, *Corporate Creativity, How Innovation and Improvement Actually Happen*, Berrett-Koehler Publishers, Inc.pp. 68-72.

When Patterson lived in his employees' working conditions, he realized how demoralizing they were. When he was on the factory floor, elbow-to-elbow with his employees, amid the noise and turmoil of production work, he learned their real concerns and motivations. Then, he took corrective action. If Patterson had kept his desk in the executive suite, he may have never fully understood why his people were sabotaging his products and may not have made the necessary changes.

When an innovator is working by him or herself, co-location is clearly unnecessary, but the process of innovation is generally not an individual activity. Typically, it requires teamwork. Co-location is crucial, especially at the start of new ventures. Words can be sent by letters and e-mail, voice intonation can be heard on the telephone, and visual cues can be seen on closed-circuit television, but for innovation nothing takes the place of being together physically to establish the essential element of trust.

The flood of ideas generated during brainstorming sessions demonstrates how physical proximity can stimulate new ideas. Idea generation by telephone, e-mail, and computer software networking has proved effective, but not nearly so productive as being physically together.

One client was talking about a joint venture he was negotiating. All the business information was in place and it seemed to make perfectly good sense, but he had some reservations. When asked what more was needed to close the deal, he said, "I need to know the person." When asked to explain, he said, "Well, I need to meet his family. If the person brings the family and introduces them, I get more comfortable. If I am invited to their home and see the way they live, I get even more comfortable. If his life is consistent, inside and outside of work, if he treats his family the same way he treats people at work, I will get even more comfortable. If the person volunteers to me that they have the same vision I have without my stating my vision first, I'm still more comfortable."

When business partners know each other personally, their ventures have a better chance of success. Once the trust is established, electronic communication is an important tool for continued discussions and trust maintenance.

The number of ideas generated from an originator-assisted system (Chapter 3) proved to be directly proportional to the location of the innovation advocate. When the originator was in close proximity to the innovation advocate, she could stop in to discuss an idea (See Figure 5.1). A study at the Office of Innovation at Kodak revealed that most of the ideas submitted came from people close to the office. There was a consistent ratio of about 40 submissions per site, per year.

Figure 5.1: The Effectiveness of Co-location

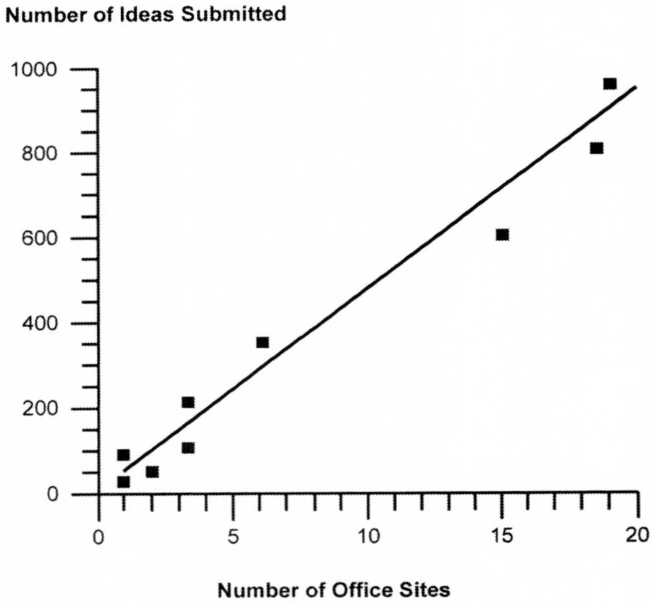

Number of Ideas Submitted

Number of Office Sites

The number of ideas submitted to the Office of Innovation was directly proportional to the number of office sites, where each office site had its own innovation advocate. If more than one innovation advocate was located at a single site, the number of ideas produced was significantly fewer per advocate.

For example, when analyzing active cases in a given timeframe, it was found that 20 ideas came from the same floor where the office was located and only one from a different floor. The physical location of the office site played an important role in the number of ideas that were submitted. Another office was opened in a different building, yet in close proximity to the first office. One advocate serviced both offices, spending equal amounts of time in each office. Each office was within the main traffic flow for the building. Almost immediately after the second office was opened, there were more than 20 more active ideas from the new location.

It did not work the other way around. When the number of advocates in one office was increased, the only thing that happened was that the number of ideas per advocate decreased. It was not the number of advocates that determines the number of ideas submitted; instead, it was office accessibility. At the same time, accessibility is not everything. Once a relationship was established, an originator would drive 45 minutes to see an advocate he had worked with before, even if another innovation advocate was down the hall. A new originator would only go to an advocate that was nearby. Established relationships survived separation.

Managing Co-Location

The message to innovation leaders is simple. The need for co-location is often acknowledged, but rarely implemented. Arrangements should be made so that people who are working jointly on an idea can work in close proximity, at least during the initial phase of a project.

There are many reasons for offices being set up in certain ways: power and prestige call for a corner office; ease of client access includes proximity to the entrance; space restraints and efficiency needs demand attention as does access to related functions. Co-location needs to be a part of the formula.

The key to the importance of co-location is its role in fostering trust and real communication between co-workers. Clearly, putting people together doesn't always bring about instant harmony. Sometimes personalities are simply different, and there is a lack of understanding—at times to the point of rising irritation—because of this difference. Antagonistic people can be agitated by proximity and sometimes there is no ready will to resolve differences. If left unchecked, such situations can be extremely destructive to a work environment. Here again, it is the role of the innovation leader to be sensitive to the differences between people and help them work out their problems. Co-location is too important to abandon because of these kinds of differences. Once again, problems should be seen as catalysts for new ideas, as the grains of sand that give rise to pearls.

How much co-location is needed? That depends on the quality of communication and the level of trust that an organization wishes to establish. People process information differently and have various ways of communicating and building trust. Trust is acquired, among other ways, through co-location. When differences between people are viewed as complementary qualities, they provide enormous benefits. When viewed as antagonistic characteristics, they can destroy the organization. Learning to leverage differences is the next challenge for the innovation leader.

CHAPTER 6

Leverage Differences

*No two men can be found who can be said to be outwardly
and inwardly united.*

*—Bahá'u'lláh (1817-1892),
Prophet Founder, The Bahá'í Faith.*

*When divergent approaches are brought together, they
can be a blessing or a curse. When used in constructive
ways, differences are a boon to innovation. This chapter
examines language, currency, cognitive, cultural, and
gender differences and their role in enhancing and
sustaining the innovation process.*

The differences that normally divide people can be
viewed in different ways. They can even be seen as
diverse perspectives and capabilities with
constructive potential. When people move beyond fear,
suspicion, mistrust, and prejudice, differences can be leveraged
to complement one another.

Two lessons about cultural differences became apparent to
me while I was working on a device to help combat fraud.

The first lesson was that how things are understood depends more on values and backgrounds than on the words used. The other was that when it is possible to get beyond the problems caused by differences, each group has something of potential value to offer the other.

While working at Kodak, I started being intrigued by how security systems worked. This wasn't my job, but I found myself toying with various ideas. I was looking for a foolproof way to identify people. Knowing that no two sets of palm prints were the same, I reasoned there should be some way to check people's palm prints for positive identification. This led to the idea of using a scanner to "read" a person's palm lines and compare them to a card that contained palm-print information. If the scan matched the information on the card, the person was positively identified. If the scan didn't match, the person didn't pass.

The next step was to make a prototype. I built a large box to hold the mechanism with a read-out of colored diodes. When there was a match, the green light would go on. If there was no match, the red light would go on. I painted the box black to hold down reflections, and, proud of my creation, I was ready to show it to some people in marketing.

When I met with the people from marketing, I made what I thought was an excellent and thorough explanation of the technology and told them how this device could be used in banks and other places. The marketing people didn't pay much attention to the technical talk. They kept looking at the box. When I was done, someone said, "I don't like the color." Another chimed in, "besides, it's too big." I protested that this was just the prototype—that the size and color were not important, it could be made smaller and it could be painted any color they wanted, but they didn't hear me. They kept talking about the color and the size. They completely missed what I said.

My first reaction was anger. "How could they be so stupid!" Then, it dawned on me that they were not stupid. They were bright, competent people who just saw the world differently. As a technical person, interested in technology and what makes things work, I focused on my interest. They were marketing people interested in positioning products for sales. Their thoughts would be "Who will buy it?" And, "Why would they want to buy it?" They had a different professional culture and mindset. We all were using English, but speaking different languages.

With a second flash of insight I realized that we were not only different, but also that we needed each other. They could market, but didn't care that much about the technical end of things, and I didn't understand sales.

Combining expertise enables people to take advantage of others' strengths and differences to achieve a common objective. This process means more than removing barriers created by differences. It means using those differences advantageously. I call this the four Cs: *Constructively Combining Complementary Capabilities.*

With this new insight I presented the idea again in **their** language and currency. They didn't like my big box, so I built a small one that had nothing but a switch hooked up to green and red diodes. It was stained to show the wood grain. They were shown the box and told it was built to fit in a bank teller's window.

A customer could come up to a teller in a bank and place a hand on the device. I inserted a fake card, put my hand on the box, turned on the green light and said, "See, this passes." A marketing staff member was asked to put her hand on the device. Another fake card was place in the box and the red light was turned on. I said, "This one didn't pass."

They said, "Hey, this is great! It's about the right size, and I really like that wood grain. Now, how do you use it?" There was no deception. They wanted to know what it would do, not how it worked.

That was 20 years ago. Today, most technical people are aware of the cultural differences within organizations, and try to have a discussion with the ultimate user early on. For me, it was both a culture shock and a valuable lesson.

Language

How many people speak the same language even when
they speak the same language?

—*Russel Hoban (1925-), American writer.*

Every working group develops its own technical language
or jargon. The terms of such a language have meaning for
them and set them apart from those who are not part of their
group. The common vocabulary also defines their values as
well as influencing how they think and process information.

Learning the language of others eases communications with
people of different organizational cultures. *This is critical to success
for the innovation leader.* Anyone who doesn't know or realize the
differences in various languages will be seen as an outsider.

The use of initials and acronyms often identifies the group
to which people belong. The ease with which acronyms like
P&L (profit and loss statements), R&D (research and
development), and MBTI (Myers-Briggs Type Indicator—see
page 94) are understood by someone says a lot about a person.

One phrase can mean different things to different groups. Critical
mass is what a chemist calls the stage when enough of a chemical is
added to a solution to change the composition. For a physicist, critical
mass is the point where a reaction sustains itself. In epidemiology,
critical mass is what a virus reaches right before the "tipping point"
of a full-blown epidemic;[33] in sales, it is the number of people needed
to buy a product to make it profitable; and a political activist sees it as
when enough people champion a cause to propel it forward.

Proprietary terms involve more than just special words. Those
who are not part of a group, such as consultants and people from
other divisions, may learn the words, but they won't be able to
communicate unless they capture the mindset behind the words.

---

[33]   See Malcolm Gladwell, *The Tipping Point: How Little Things Can Make a Big*
Difference, 2002.

Nonverbal Communication

Nonverbal communicationalso varies from group to group. Being able to interpret non-verbal cues effectively is important because they reflect important subtleties of that sub-culture.

A young, muscular schoolteacher (he had just returned from the Marine Corps) got a job teaching in a difficult inner city high-school class that had a reputation for being rowdy, belligerent, and especially hard on new teachers. The first day of class, he walked to the front of the room, took off his jacket, tie, and shirt, turned his back to his students, and, without saying a word, flexed his muscles. He turned around, faced the class, dressed, and asked if there were any questions. There were none; he had no disciplinary problems.

I traveled throughout Europe with a friend from southern France, Jean Weck. As we went from country to country, Jean would seem to change physically. His gestures and even the way he walked would take on the mannerisms typical of the area we were in. Although he did not always speak the language of the places we visited, he looked and acted like the local people. When I described what I saw, Jean was surprised because he was not aware of it. He said, "You're right, I *do* do that." Jean had traveled extensively and worked intimately with people in many countries. His subconscious actions demonstrate a sensitivity that goes beyond words and says, in effect, "I am with you and have a deep desire to understand you."

This interest and respect cannot be faked. People can detect the subtle nuances of non-verbal communication. Jean communicated effectively because of his sincere respect for those around him. If a person's motives are self-serving, there will be little sense of trust and therefore a poor connection.

Nonverbal communication also has a role in high-level and formal negotiations. Toward the end of the Cold War, delicate negotiations were taking place between the United States and the Soviet Union regarding a weapons issue. A courteous handshake was part of the routine when the two negotiating teams came together each day. One of the members of the Soviet team shook hands with everyone, but when shaking hands with the female members of the U.S. team, he squeezed their hands so hard that it caused great pain. Two women on the team complained to others in their delegation. It was determined that the handshake action was clearly meant as a negotiating technique designed to intimidate. In discussing how to deal with the situation, a formal complaint was ruled out because there was a danger it could escalate the incident and impair negotiations. Instead, they decided to send a direct, informal, nonverbal, but clear message.

During a subsequent meeting, when both delegations were greeting each other with the usual handshakes, a muscular American colonel shook hands with the offending Soviet in such a way that he deliberately dislocated the man's knuckles. With that clearly communicated gesture, negotiations proceeded on even terms. After the Cold War, the two hand shakers had an opportunity to speak to each other. The Russian told the American that he understood exactly why the American did what he did. There were no hard feelings and the handshake was not taken personally. It was strictly business.[34]

> *I speak Spanish to God, Italian to women, French to men*
> *and German to my horse.*
>
> —*Charles I of Spain (1500-1558),*
> *Charles V of the Holy Roman Empire.*

A number of years ago, a colleague asked me how he could convince people in corporate headquarters of the value of an idea he had. His attempts at talking to them had so far been unsuccessful. I told him, "You have to talk to them through

---

[34] Personal interview with a member of the American team, who asked to remain anonymous.

their neckties, because their ties are connected to their ears."
He didn't understand what I meant. I explained that unless
he wore a necktie, they wouldn't understand what he was
talking about. If he put on a tie, and dressed the way they
did, they would be able to hear him.

Following that advice, my colleague bought a tie and a
suit and went to corporate headquarters dressed in a manner
appropriate for that culture. He came back elated. This time
they listened, understood and accepted his idea. Previously,
his clothing had set him so much apart that no one took him
or his idea seriously. The decision-makers were probably not
consciously aware that the way a person dressed would make
any difference in their decisions.

Currency

> *The cost of a thing is the amount of what I call life which*
> *is required to be exchanged for it.*
>
> *—Henry David Thoreau (1817-1862),*
> *American writer and philosopher.*

What is currency? It is a medium of exchange and a method
for establishing relative importance. But, not all people value
the same things the same way. In this society, we all use money,
but money is not the only currency. Some people value power,
peer acceptance, political influence, or organizational growth
more than money.

Numbers measure different things in different ways,
reflecting different mindsets. For financial people, numbers
are generally related to money and are used to measure the
progress of the company. Terms such as revenues, pre-tax or
after-tax profits, P&L, profit margins, loss ratios, and so on
are part of the vocabulary. For someone in research and
development, the number of patents and publications are
important indicators of success. People in production want to

know the number of units produced and the ratio of rejections or returns. People in sales may be more focused on the size and number of orders, the number of customers being served, new markets, and quotas.

People who are visually oriented gain considerable information from numbers on a graph or chart. For verbal people, an oral or written explanation is preferred. Some are both visually and verbally oriented. These differences have nothing to do with intelligence or capabilities. They are just different ways to access information and communicate in ways that are meaningful.

Because people have diverse values, rewards are the most meaningful when they are in the currency of the people receiving them. For example, people in sales love contests. They have been known to produce thousands of dollars in new sales to win a contest with a prize that's worth a small fraction of what is earned from the sales. When you reward people with things that are important to you, but not to them, the reward will not have the desired effect; in some cases, it might even be insulting.

Marty had risen in the finance department of a large company. When the company did some restructuring, he found himself at the head of a sales division. During his first year, the company went through a financial slump, and he canceled the annual sales meeting. His salespeople told him he shouldn't do that, but he didn't hear them. He viewed the meeting from the standpoint of his financial culture, and did not see its importance to the people in sales. He reasoned that the information normally shared at the meeting could be communicated through memos, and the sales meeting was a needless expense.

What Marty did not realize was that, for the sales team, this meeting was the high point of the year. This was a time when their achievements were paraded before their peers, and they got the kind of recognition that was most meaningful to them. It was also a time when they exchanged and explored new ideas related to sales. At these meetings, sales-people would get excited about their products in a way not possible through memos. Marty's mistake was costly. What he communicated to his department was that he was not one of them. He trivialized something of great importance to the sales force. The result was disastrous. Sales dropped. The sales force felt betrayed, and didn't trust Marty, which caused lingering problems.

Cognition

When two people think exactly the same way, one of them is superfluous.

—Unknown Origin

Cognition is the mental process or faculty of knowing, including such aspects as awareness, perception, reasoning, and judgment. Cognitive differences are the varied ways in which people view the world, access and process information. From Hippocrates in 450 BC to Carl Jung and beyond, these differences have been recognized, classified, and analyzed. The innovation leader acknowledges that the differences between people are real, and understands that such differences are invaluable tools for the innovation process when they are leveraged.

By recognizing cognitive differences, it is possible to encourage people according to their strengths and use the style that is natural for them. By valuing different styles, "out-of-the-box" thinkers can be focused on developing breakthrough concepts. At the same time, people oriented to detail are needed to connect wild ideas with reality.

There are many reputable instruments that can assess people's cognitive styles, help them gain a better understanding of different thinking processes, and allow them to work together effectively. Two effective instruments are the Myers-Briggs Type Indicator (MBTI™)and the Kirton Adaptation-Innovation Inventory (KAI™).

The MBTI™ is based on the psychological theories of Carl Jung (1875-1961), who identified various predictable patterns of human behavior.

Figure 6.1: Myers-Briggs Type Indicator (MBTI)

Scale	Personality Preferences	
Where Energy Comes From	Extroversion: Preference for drawing energy from the outside world of people, activities, or things	Introversion: Preference for drawing energy from one's internal world of ideas, emotions, or impressions
How We Gather Information	Sensing: Preference for taking in information through the five senses and noticing what is actual	Intuition: Preference for taking in information through a "sixth sense" and noticing what might be
How We Make Decisions	Thinking: Preference for organizing and structuring information to decide in a logical, objective way	Feeling: Preference for organizing and structuring information to decide in a personal, value-oriented way
How We Live in the Outer World	Judging: Preference for living in a planned and organized way	Perceiving: Preference for living a spontaneous and flexible life

Introduction to Type in Organizations, Second Edition
Sandra Krebs Hirsh
Jean M. Kurnmerow 1987

Inspired by the work of psychologist Carl Jung, the Myers-Briggs Type Indicator (MBTI), provides a useful measure of personality by looking at eight personality preferences. These eight preferences are organized into four bipolar scales. When taking the MBTI, the four preferences that a person identifies as most like him—or herself (one from each of the four scales) are combined into a type. Reprinted with permission from Sandra Krebs-Hirsh and Jean M. Kurnmerow.

This instrument is a questionnaire. The results adapt Jung's theory of psychological types to the workplace and everyday life by describing cognitive differences. A proper appreciation of the nature and value of the differences is a powerful tool for effective communications.

My chief of staff, Janet Meier, and I were meeting with representatives of our Philadelphia branch and a potential new branch member. I spent about 40 minutes unsuccessfully trying to explain how something was marketed. Realizing I wasn't being clear, I asked Janet to explain it. The other person got the idea in about three minutes. The difference was that Janet and the other person had similar cognitive profiles; both had similar problem-solving styles and ways of taking in information and making decisions. They could understand each other easily.

Does that mean that one type is better or smarter than the other? No. It just means that differences exist and they need to be taken into account when people are attempting to understand one another.

There are many times when a full range of approaches is desired. When you mix people with different cognitive styles, you increase the possibility of confusion and the risk of miscommunication. At the same time, you enlarge the range of possible benefits because of supplementary insights and thinking patterns. If you understand how to work together effectively, you appreciate and crave the differences.

The difference can be compared to the use of light. When a full spectrum is needed for complete illumination, diversity is essential. A narrow, intense beam produces a special function and becomes a laser. The same principle applies to organizations. For a breadth of ideas, a full range or spectrum of thinking is best. For focused concentration, grouping people with similar styles is the most effective.

I was on the board of directors of a small organization and had all sorts of wild ideas. One of the other board members, Ray, was just the opposite and I considered him "risk adverse." We were tolerant of each other. Ray would let me go until I went too far out of line, then he'd start to raise objections. At the same time, Ray could see possibilities that would never otherwise occur to him. Between us, we came up with many projects that were practical and workable. It wasn't until Ray was no longer on the board that I realized how important he was to me. Ray would rein me in when needed. This gave me the freedom to have completely wild ideas. When Ray was no longer there, I had to self-censor my ideas. That severely limited my freedom to think in novel ways.

Sometimes, there are advantages to putting together people with similar styles. Idea Connections was called in as an outside consultant to an oil company that needed to develop new strategies for oil exploration—a problem they had grappled with for more than 20 years. We assembled two groups. One was a group of external experts from various disciplines who had similar cognitive profiles. (They were "out-of-the-box" thinkers.) These experts were not told their cognitive styles were similar. They were mixed with a group of internal experts who were also "out-of-the-box" thinkers. The entire group was exposed to a variety of new experiences, including meditation, to quiet and open up their minds.

In three days they achieved a breakthrough that had eluded them for years. There were two major factors. One was that the groups' similarities in cognitive style helped them trust one another on a fundamental level. This enabled them to get involved in the break-through deeply and rapidly because they had an intuitive understanding of each other. They easily entered unknown experiences with a spirit of camaraderie.

The other major factor was the intimate acquaintance with the problem from inside the organization blending, with trust and amity, with fresh approaches from outside the group. The insiders knew what would not work, but that knowledge can also act as a blinder. At the same time, the outsiders had an appreciation and comprehension of the objective.

Another time we were asked to work with a very talented group from Information Systems (IS) in a major corporation. This group's job was to create the next stage of development for an IS system (a breakthrough). They had presented many good ideas to their senior management, but the reception was disappointing. The first thing we did was administer the KAI™ (Figure 6.2), created by psychologist, Michael Kirton, in 1976.

Figure 6.2: Your Relative KAI Position

Adaptor	Innovator
Efficient, thorough, enterprising, adaptable, methodical, organized, precise, reliable, dependable	Ingenious, original, energetic, individualistic, independent, unconventional, spontaneous, thinks tangentially
Accepts problem definition	Challenges problem definition
Makes "goals" of the "means"	Does things differently
Concerned with resolving problems rather than finding them	Questions or disregards the "means"
Seeks solutions to problems in tried and understood ways	Discovers problems and avenues for their solutions
Reduces problems by improvement and greater efficiency, while aiming at continuity and stability	Manipulates problems by questioning existing assumptions; is catalyst to settled groups, irreverent of their consensual views
Seems impervious to boredom, seems able to maintain high accuracy in long spells of detailed work	Capable of detailed routine work (systems maintenance) for only short bursts; quick to delegate routine tasks
Is an authority within given structures	Tends to take control in unstructured situations
High Adaptors and Innovators Are Often Seen by the Other Side as...	
Dogmatic, compliant, stuck in a "rut," timid, conforming, and inflexible	Unsound, impractical, abrasive, undiciplined, insensitive, and one who loves to create confusion

Adapted from Michael Kirton, "Adaptors and Innovators: A Description and Measure," *Journal of Applied Psychology*, 1976, 61, pp.622-629

Reprinted with permission from Michael Kirton.

Adaption-Innovation theory states that people differ in their style of problem solving, decision-making, and creativity. The KAI (Kirton Adaption/Innovation Inventory) is a measure of style, not capacity. It is an indicator of how you prefer to solve problems, not of your level of problem-solving skill. Some individuals will prefer an adaptive approach (e.g., they are "paradigm builders"), while others will prefer an innovative approach (e.g., they are "paradigm breakers"). Your score reflects your preferred style. Whatever it is, it is neither "good" nor "bad," "right" nor "wrong." Groups require a diversity of styles to optimize their functioning. Each style has its own strengths and, of course, its potential weaknesses. The purpose of the KAI is to help you better understand your own and other people's problem-solving style preferences and likely behavior patterns, which in turn help to produce more effective individual and team performance.

This instrument indicates the manner in which people are creative. It does not tell how creative they are—it tells only if they prefer to do things "better," or do them "differently." After administering the test to the IS group, it became clear why this group could not be understood. Their average KAI™ score indicated that this was a group that abhorred structure and preferred to find solutions that were novel and unique (extreme paradigm pioneers/innovators). They preferred to do things differently. The group's manager had a similar score. On the other hand, the members of the management team the group reported to had scores that indicated that they preferred order and did not like things that seemed unorthodox (midrange paradigm builders/adaptors). After explaining the difference in cognitive styles that various people have, I pointed out that the problem between them was one of communication not substance. It had to do with their different styles. It was made clear that the IS group did not have to change their ideas; what they needed to change was how they presented them to an audience that processed things differently. There was a member of the group, Frank, whose KAI™ score was closer to that of the management team score than any of the others. I suggested that Frank could act as an interpretations coach between the IS group and the management team. Frank should review all presentations first. The members of the group would never have selected Frank for this purpose, because he was not that highly regarded, and certainly was not their most "creative" member. If Frank understood the presentation and coached their manager, the manager would be able to explain it to the IS group's management team in a way they would understand.

From then on, every presentation made was not only understood, but implemented. Both management and the IS group thought the other group had become smarter and had finally gotten the point. The IS group learned to speak another language and a key learning occurred: it is everyone's job to speak other people's cognitive language, not ask them to learn yours.

Culture

> Culture is the name for what people are interested in, their thoughts, their models, the books they read and the speeches they hear, their table-talk, gossip, controversies, historical sense and scientific training, the values they appreciate, the quality of life they admire. All communities have a culture. It is the climate of their civilization
>
> —Walter Lipton (1889-1974), American journalist.

Ethnicity and heritage shape the way people view the world and how they react. There are subtleties of meaning that are sometimes hard for others to understand no matter how well intentioned. These are expressed emotionally, rather than logically.

The innovation leader knows that differences can enhance the process of innovation. Diversity is "starter yeast" for innovative ideas. People in every group have developed unique and valuable characteristics. By using the full span of contributions, wonderful new ideas can emerge. Prejudice, and thinking in terms of stereotypes, gets in the way of innovation. As a result, an enormous reservoir of ideas is sacrificed.

When a large cosmetics company made an attempt to penetrate the African-American market, it failed miserably. It was not until they involved African Americans in the design of the cosmetics and in the marketing strategy that they succeeded. If an organization wants to be global, it needs to have people inside the organization who understand and have been part of the markets being pursued. It is reasonable to ask, "Why can't that be done by hiring people from outside the company?" The answer is simple. It takes someone who understands both the culture of the organization and that of the target population. In a sense, that individual must be bilingual—speaking both languages—and so becomes a bridge between the two.

Many companies have had diversity training, yet it has been effective for only a few. Members of my company surveyed reports of diversity training to find out what worked and what did not work. What they discovered was that diversity training is effective when the upper echelons of the organization are committed to its success. Unum Life Insurance Company of America is one such company.[35] After diversity training, a Caucasian employee excitedly reported that it was the best thing that ever happened. Employees discovered that the fears expressed between groups were really fears everyone had. By reaching out to differences, they touched a core of human commonality. Since the training, people of all backgrounds had a better understanding of themselves and there was much better interaction throughout the organization. It happened because the President, Stephen B. Center, made it happen. He was committed to its success and spent considerable time and energy communicating this commitment to the entire company.

The head of a large law firm told me that he wanted diversity in his firm, but could not find qualified people. I asked him

---

[35]   Stephen B. Center, "The Diversity Journey," *Human Resource Professional*, issue 307, July 12, 1996, pp. 3-7.

what the people looked like that he talked to when he needed help. At first he did not seem to understand until I pointed out that, if all the people he confided in looked like him, he would never achieve the diversity he was seeking. He finally realized that he had to live the quest for diversity in his own life before he could expect to see it happen in his law firm. Success depends on a consistent and strong commitment, starting at the top, vigorously backed at all levels of management.

Gender

Traditionally, many companies have made the mistake of having men design products for women to buy. When women are "in" on the design of women's products, the products have much more sales appeal because women know the subtleties that men might not consider.

For example, men usually design public buildings. Men's and women's rest rooms are generally designed to be equal in size with the same number of fixtures in each. But go to any concert hall or sporting arena where the men's and women's facilities are "equal" and during intermission, there will be a much longer line in front of the women's rest rooms than the men's. Why? For many reasons (biological, psychological, and sociological) women need more time to use the facilities than men. To be fair, the measure should not be the number of units per person, but the number of units based on time. Women architects know the difference. Men generally have to have it pointed out to them, and even then, not all are able to see its significance or take it seriously.

Managing Differences

Knowing how to properly leverage differences in ways that are fair, open, and honest is probably the greatest challenge for an innovation leader. Anything that seems exploitative or patronizing will backfire. Anything pursued without conviction is doomed. When there is a genuine belief that people from all groups have something of value to offer and when everyone is respected as a worthy human being, then the innovation leader can leverage differences for undreamed of benefits. Sincerity, energy, and sensitivity are the innovation leader's best tools. Following are key points to remember when managing the cultural differences we discussed earlier in this chapter.

Language. While it is important to be comfortable with the multiple languages within the organization, it is just as important to acquaint people from different parts of the organization with the particular terms of innovation. Words, such as champion, sponsor, sifting, originator, and others, are part of the special vocabulary of innovation. These are not vague or general descriptors, but have specific, technical meanings, which are lost unless there is a working knowledge of the language of innovation. (See Appendix B.)

Currencies. Managing the different currencies of the organization starts with understanding different values among people. The best way to do this is through observation and deducing what is of value to others. For example, by observation you may learn that a valued researcher cannot remember the market size of her project or isn't sure who is the head of sales. However, she may know all the steps needed to get patents. Then, you know where her head and heart are and what is considered important.

Reward and motivation are best when geared to special items of significance for each group. For some people, a plaque of commendation is very meaningful. Others regard it as environmentally wasteful and an expenditure that would have been better used for equipment or a bonus.

When someone has to present an idea to a potential sponsor, the innovation leader can play an important role in how the idea will be heard. He can help the idea originator know something about the language, currency, cognitive styles, and culture of the person to whom the idea is being presented.

This can be done best by giving examples and role-playing exercises. That way, when the individual is talking with potential sponsors, he will have a greater chance of being heard and understood.

As mentioned earlier, there have been many studies on cognitive styles. The innovation leaders of today can access useful insights and instruments to gain a deeper understanding of cognitive differences, and better leverage peoples' relative strengths within the organization or an innovation project.

By understanding cognitive diversities, it is possible to encourage people according to their strengths. People are most comfortable and effective when they can use the style that is natural for them. Different jobs require skills that are more conducive to some styles than others. It is the innovation leader's job to recognize this reality and to encourage people in the direction of their natural inclinations. It is also a requirement of an innovation leader to be fluent in all these styles. Trying to force different people into the same mold produces both inferior results and frustration. A person may cope but it will take its toll in the form of added stress.

Physio-cultural. The best way to appreciate differences of ethnicity and culture is to seek out people of various groups. Learning to know them as individuals opens windows to understanding, perspectives, hopes, fears, and aspirations, all of which are vital to using varied contributions constructively.

Gender. Conscious efforts to ignore the stereotypes of gender differences is the first step in appreciating the true value of gender-based perspectives, and understanding when they are important to the task under consideration.

Overcoming barriers. There are two ways to learn the subtleties of different groups: one is through observation and the other is by befriending a person who can explain them. I make a practice of befriending people in different areas of organizations in which I work. I discover what makes them tick, by learning how to: speak with them honestly and directly in their language; understand their cultural values; and leverage their differences through a network that goes past barriers. It should be remembered that just as practice is needed to be fluent in any non-native language, it takes practice to appreciate and utilize diversity in positive and natural ways.

By constructively combining complementary capabilities, it is possible to reverse the centuries-old tendency to treat people who are different with suspicion and mistrust. Everyone benefits from the contributions of those who see the world in other ways. A true innovation leader is one who seeks and lives by inclusion.

The preceding chapters discussed the essence of innovation concluding with leveraging differences. Now, it is time to look at the organizational side of things. To start with, there are danger signals that sound the alert when seeds of destruction begin to grow.

PART II

The Innovation Process:
Its Environment

Innovation does not happen in a vacuum. Its home is the real world with all its complications, problems, and setbacks. Growing organisms thrive best in nurturing environments, so, too, does innovation. The healthier the environment, the better the results.

The following pages outline both factors that threaten the environment of innovation and those conditions that help sustain innovation.

Attention is drawn to the following three principles:

- Destructive Elements Are Present at Creation
- Soft Values Drive the Organization
- Trust is the Means and Love the Unspoken Word

CHAPTER 7

The Elements Of Destruction Are Present At Creation

Destruction, hence, like creation, is one of Nature's mandates.

—Marquis de Sade (1740-1814), French writer.

Birth, renewal, reproduction, and death are the cycles of life. Products, processes, procedures, and new enterprises also go through cycles. Companies must continually be renewed or recede into oblivion and perish. The life of a product or procedure depends on a number of factors, some of which are within the control of leadership and some of which are not. This chapter looks at the inherent destructive elements that are part of the lifecycle of a product or a company and, as well, the elements of destruction that can be circumvented. A quality of destructive elements is that they are difficult to perceive. You cannot see, smell, or feel them. But, they are there and they are the silent killers of organizations.

Starting a new venture takes a special combination of skill and creative energy. Maintaining it takes different combinations of skill, talent, and interest that vary according to the size of the organization. These differences are more qualitative than quantitative. Just because someone has the skill and capacity to run a company at one level doesn't mean that she is capable of taking it to the next level. Many organizations have failed because they grew beyond the capacity and/or interest of the one who started it, leading to its destruction—the seed of which was present from the beginning.

Even when the founder is courageous enough to recognize personal limitations and brings others in to do whatever is necessary to maintain operational health, another seed of destruction is introduced. Just as germs and viruses are unwittingly carried from place to place by hosts, when new people bring fresh talent and new capacity to the management team, they also bring with them characteristics that may not fit in with the existing culture and are potentially destructive.

Some destructive forces are a function of time, place, or culture. An acorn planted close to a house can get its start because of the protection afforded by the house, but as it grows and its root system needs room to expand, it creates a problem for itself. The owner may cut down the tree because its roots threaten to break the foundation of the house. The danger was in the acorn.

In business, as in all aspects of life, there are elements of destruction. If detected early enough, appropriate action may be taken to counter the problem. Yet, these forces are not generally visible and are therefore hard to detect. How do you defend against potential problems of which you are not aware? One way is to be sensitive to the possibilities and where they are apt to lurk.

This is a difficult task for creative people because they are busy looking ahead, planning, building, and achieving success. The energy of growth often renders the elements of destruction dormant, but they are there, ready to take root at the first opportunity.

Success as a destructive force

A product can be so successful that it destroys its own market. Consider the story of the Model T Ford.[36] Automobiles had been playthings for the rich. Henry Ford (1863-1947) decided to make a car for under $1,000 so the working person could afford one. He wanted his factory workers to be able to buy the product they were making. Mass production was revolutionized by his relentless insistence on standardized parts, limited model changes, and better use of tools and workbench arrangements. In 1909, the first year of production for the Model T, 17,771 cars were produced; each sold for $950. By 1924, its peak year, 202,667 cars were produced. They sold for $350 each. The Model T dominated the automobile industry.[37]

This factory revolution triggered a broader economic and social upheaval. In 1910, there were 458,000 registered automobiles. A decade later there were 8 million, a 16-fold increase.[38] Once an amusement for the wealthy, they now belonged to the masses.

This success spawned new industries and brought on a need for more and better roads. Roadside services, such as service stations and roadside cabins, came into being. A used car market emerged, as well as installment buying. Ford's car not only dominated the market, it created a motorized America, and spawned new industries and financial priorities and strategies.

This gave birth to a problem that Ford had not anticipated. When the Model T became available for $350, a growing number of people decided to pay a little more to get a better

---

[36] R. J. Samuelson, "The Assembly Line," *NewsweekExtra*, Winter 1997-1998, p. 24.

[37] Ibid.

[38] Ibid.

car. Ford refused to change his tactics, and by 1925 his car had slipped to below 50% of the market share. In the next year, market share had slipped even further. "By 1927 the Model T was finished. Though the company recovered, it never regained its complete dominance. The man and his car had become victims of their own success."[39]

Several elements of destruction can be identified in this account. A major one is that Ford had a passion, if not a fixation, on providing a low-cost car. That was both the secret of his success and the seed of destruction. His low prices revolutionized not just the auto industry, but also aspects of the American culture to the point that lower and lower prices were no longer as important as they once had been. Before it went out of production, the price of the Model T had decreased to $299 and no one was buying it.

Personal relationships contain elements of destruction

When someone is put in a position of power and authority and hasn't successfully balanced personal interests with those of the company, partner, and/or employees, the predictable result is the destruction of the individual as well as the venture being led.

Joe and Archie started a partnership, in part, because of their differences. They knew the value of leveraging differences and their alliance was successful because each provided something the other lacked. After 10 years of successfully working with Archie, Joe decided to devote most of his time to other activities. They still worked together for specific projects several times a year. As Joe reduced his time in the business, however, he discovered that Archie's aggressiveness, which was an initial part of the success of the partnership, was no longer held in check by Joe's more settled manner. Greed was getting the better of Archie. When Joe was not

---

[39]   Ibid.

there to monitor their affairs, Archie started stealing business in violation of the partnership agreement. A bitter court battle resulted. A destructive element was Joe's assumption that the relationship would stay the same, even when he was not there.

The life cycle is a destructive force

> *Creation destroys as it goes, throws down one tree for the rise of another.*
>
> —D. H. Lawrence (1885-1930), British writer.

Products and procedures each have built-in limits. Not long ago, merchants needed well-organized storerooms of ample size to be sure there was enough stock available. Today, with Just in Time (JIT) shipping, little inventory is kept in the back room. Merchants who do not adjust find it difficult to compete.

The real element of destruction is the belief that a need for a product will last forever. In more recent years, the typewriter has lost its market. Twenty years ago offices were filled with an arsenal of typewriters; IBM could not make its popular Selectric® typewriters fast enough to keep up with the demand. Today, typewriters are rarely seen in any office. Typewriter keyboards live on with the computer, but may become obsolete when voice input becomes more common. The keyboard's strength is the number of people who know how to use it. A seed of destruction is the need for manual manipulation.

New processes contain destructive elements

Innovative procedures can also wreck havoc. During the 1920s and 1930s, Frederick W. Taylor's book, *The Principles of Scientific Management*,[40] came to be regarded as the bible for the new

---

[40]   Frederick Winslow Taylor, *The Principles of Scientific Management*, Harper Brothers, New York, 1911.

industrial age. Taylor is credited with the standardization and mechanization of manufacturing procedures, which reduced the amount of thinking required by workers.

His system, which became known as Taylorism, made manufacturing more efficient and had a positive effect on profitability. However, Francis Fukuyama (1952-), senior social scientist at the Rand Corporation, argues that Taylorism eroded the base of trust within companies and created a chasm between management and labor in America. He claims that much of the subsequent labor unrest was a direct result of the loss of trust that developed when workers became regarded as machines. The element of destruction was promoting efficiency at the expense of employees.[41]

It has only been in recent decades that some organizations have taken positive steps to reintroduce a level of trust and give workers renewed opportunities to participate mentally and emotionally in their work. The destructive element was the attitude toward employees. It appeared to make economic sense to treat people like machines. Profitability increased, but the real price was high. Treat people like machines and they behave like machines.

Entrepreneurial strength masks destructive forces

The energy and innovation needed to launch an enterprise will not last forever. Edwin Land (1909-1991) of Polaroid[42] was a superb entrepreneur and driver in his organization. He built a large and profitable company, but as an innovator he did not create in his company the elements needed to sustain innovation. When the founders are no longer present, huge problems emerge (over time) because the founders' energy,

---

[41]   F. Fukuyama, *Trust*, Simon and Schuster, 1995.

[42]   Robert Levering and Milton Moskowitz, "Polaroid Corporation," *The 100 Best Companies to Work for in America*, rev. ed., Currency/Doubleday, New York, 1993.

vision, entrepreneurship, and innovations that launched their companies are gone. There is nothing deliberate or sinister about this. For whatever reason, they do not implement a means for their creative energy to be replenished. Visionaries supply the creative impulse that can carry a company a long way, but the vision may die when they do.

Destructive forces are hidden in the founders' strengths. Although they may be energetic, ingenious, and innovative, many don't understand the full extent of the contribution they make to the success and growth of the company. Founders are so focused on innovation and growth that they may pay little attention to continuing that growth beyond their lives. Like Land, they may be unaware of the unique, personal characteristics they had that were essential for their success, and that the loss of these factors would cause problems. Fortunately for Land, he had both enough energy and financial resources to recover, regain strength, and rebuild. More often, however, companies flounder when they lose their founders.

The paradigm of success is a destructive force

Other companies have not been so fortunate. Forty car companies were featured during the first National Automobile Show in New York City in 1900.[43] Many of them were highly successful, but how many are left from the original list? After WW II, there were numerous passenger service airlines. Few are left today. Most of the successful companies in both of these industries were dependent on the energy of their originators and were vulnerable when that energy was gone.

The Sears and Roebuck story provides several examples of the need to make adjustments.[44] During the Depression, Sears' legendary catalog became an American institution. Times

---

[43]   R.J. Samuelson, op. cit., p. 20

[44]   D. Sun, "Sears, Roebuck and Co.," *Company Histories: Vol. V*, in Adele Hast, ed., St James Press, Chicago, 1991, pp. 180-183.

changed, and the catalog sales, which had been their staple, went down; the "big book" was no longer profitable. The board of directors made the tough decision to abandon the catalog, which had been the company's pride for nearly a century.

In addition to catalog sales, Sears had strength in its many stores in the small towns throughout America. After WW II, the company anticipated the movement away from small towns and into suburbs. It changed its development strategy. Before the proliferation of shopping malls, Sears started building large stores just outside the big cities. The commercial activity in small towns dropped sharply, but to a large extent, Sears was out of that market before it collapsed.[45]

The Montgomery Ward Company started about the same time as Sears and was their major competitor in the catalog business.[46] After WW II, their dynamic, strong-willed leader, Sewell Avery (1874-1960), who had a genius for buying when prices were low, stuck to the methods that had made the company successful. Yet, this was also an element of destruction because Avery did not question his basic assumptions. He was convinced that a major depression would follow the war— historically true. He knew it was time to expand, but he delayed expansion so he could take advantage of the anticipated depression. He reasoned that he could build new stores at reduced costs while his competitor, Sears, would have built during high prices. He anticipated that Sears would have difficulty recovering its expansion cost and would be hurt by the depression, while Avery and his organization, by waiting, could outdistance Sears and do it at bargain prices. The depression did not come and Sears, not Ward, became the nation's leading retailer.[47] Avery's element of destruction was his assumption that economic history would repeat itself.

---

[45]   Ibid.

[46]   J. Wankoff, "Montgomery Ward & Co., Incorporated," *Company Histories*, op. cit., pp. 145-148.

[47]   Ibid.

When Sears departed from what had made it great, it escaped a force of destruction that was inherent in its origin. When Ward continued the strategies that had made it great, it became a victim of an element of destruction. Ward is gone while Sears is venturing into another risky challenge, that of small-town, owner-operated stores.[48]

Managing the elements of destruction

It is difficult, or perhaps impossible, to manage the elements of destruction. The best anyone can do is to be aware of them without dwelling on them. When a seed of destruction is detected, appropriate action can be taken.

Profitability masks the seed of destruction lurking behind a rosy picture of strong profits. Willingness to make changes in the light of success, to be responsive and to continually innovate, is an essential trait for avoiding the scourge of destructive forces.

The best way to ward off destruction is to create an environment where change and innovation flourish. Beneath the tangible assets of an organization are soft values. These are the values that actually drive the organization. Both the quantity and quality of innovation is dependent upon the nature of the soft values. That is why understanding them is so important.

---

[48] D. Sun, op. cit.

CHAPTER 8

Soft Values Drive The Organization

Every true man, sir, who is a little above the level of the beasts and plants does not live for the sake of living . . . but he lives so as to give a meaning and a value to his own life.

*—Luigi Pirandello (1867-1936),
Italian dramatist and novelist.*

Hard values are results, like the scores and statistics of sports. Soft values have to do with how the game is played. Soft values constitute the soul of an organization. They are the essence of what drives a company. They are the building blocks generating wisdom and motivation.

The best way to understand soft values is to compare them with hard values, which measure things that have a physical presence. Hard values relate to the company's financial strength and include revenues, assets, the balance sheet, dividend history, profitability, and stock value. Quarterly and annual reports and the company's prospectus reflect hard values.

Soft values are more difficult to measure. They include a range of more subtle items, such as motivation, how people feel about themselves and their company, and how they interact with and treat one another. Soft values form the basis for an instinctive feeling of what is good or bad, or right or wrong. They foster pride in one's work, trustworthiness, camaraderie, and a sense of fair play. They can also produce an indifferent, or even hostile attitude toward the organization.

While we talk about hard values, like the scores and statistics of an athletic event, it is the things that happen on the playing field—the soft values—that put scores on the board. A major league quarterback was asked by a sportscaster to comment on his team's statistics and scores, and to make projections about future games. The quarterback responded, "That's for you guys to worry about. I just concentrate on the game."

Like the sportscaster, traditional executives are oriented toward hard values. That knowledge is essential, but only part of the story. Soft values produce the results that hard values measure. They drive the company and make it work. Ironically, they are often considered fringe issues and not important to the financial strength of the organization.

One way to gain perspective is to look at how hard and soft values apply to a country. The hard values of a country include measurements like the Gross Domestic Product, strength of its currency, balance of trade, its geographic size and location. But these numbers do not convey a country's culture, spirit, or its unique identity. In order to understand those things, you need to know about its people: their history, hopes, dreams, and fears; what makes them proud, happy, or sad; how they treat their children and their elderly; their educational priorities; and whether the streets are safe and clean.

Citizens of the United States are not motivated by reports of the Gross Domestic Product, and they are either angered or turned off when the national debt is mentioned. Corny though it may sound, what appeals to most citizens are patriotism and their love of country. The years 1983 through 1986 included the centennial year for the Statue of Liberty. During that time, this symbol of the United States underwent massive rehabilitation, involving expensive replacement of the statue's leaky glass and metal torch with one made of gilded copper. Millions were raised for this project and for the Ellis Island restoration by massive voluntary contributions. No amount of rhetoric would motivate those same people to donate that much money to reduce the national debt or make up for the deficit in the balance of trade.

On September 11, 2001, Americans received a devastating blow. After the destruction of the World Trade Towers, the country, shaken to its core, awakened to a new set of global realities. We saw that we are not universally beloved in the world and could not help but ask why. At its heart, America, because of this awful tragedy, is coming to realize that the caring and connectedness we have for each other must extend out to the human family as a whole.

The people in an organization are also primarily motivated by their culture. These are soft values, not hard values. Culture is made up of two parts: 1) behaviors, and 2) the values that underlie those behaviors. This can be compared to an iceberg. What you see above the water are the behaviors (organizational practices). The values and motives are below the water. They are not visible, but they underlie the behaviors and, like an iceberg, comprise the bulk of the culture.

Figure 8.1: The Iceberg

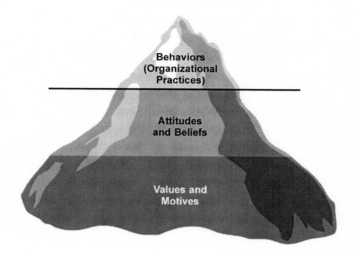

Organizational behaviors are like the tip of the iceberg—above the waterline and visible. Like most of the iceberg, the bulk of the organizational culture (including the attitudes, beliefs, values, and motivations that support behaviors) is not visible.

The importance of culture rarely is more obvious than during acquisitions and mergers. The more similar the cultures, the better the chance of success. When the cultures are very different, the probability of success is lower, even when the merger or acquisition appears to make good business sense otherwise. The reasons are not hard to identify. The respective work forces have difficulty understanding one another; they have different priorities and objectives, and there is less foundation for trust. Experts in the field of mergers and acquisitions always consider cultural differences and their many ramifications before suggesting that a deal be consummated. Many of the problems Daimler Chrysler is now facing have their roots in the cultural differences of the original companies. This is analogous to a ship approaching an iceberg. The ship faces more damage from the ice below the waterline than it is from the ice above it.

Understanding soft values

If hard values are those values that concern the clear and ever-present bottom line, soft values are the ones that, at a deep level, give direction to work-a-day activities. In organizations, the most important soft values can serve to focus vision, enhance self-improvement, and open the possibilities for innovation. Their negative components form an atmosphere that is not conducive to the creation of direction and new ideas.

In any organization, some of the positive characteristics of soft values are: purity of motive, spirit, open-mindedness, camaraderie, humility, patience and long-suffering, and service. On the other hand, the negative characteristics of soft values that also have an effect on organizations are: contentiousness, stubbornness, pride, discounting, indiscriminate criticism, and a dominating attitude.

The following section outlines some of the soft values that should be well understood.

SOFT VALUES THAT WORK

Motive

While it is true that without money and capital, organizations cannot succeed, it is also true that the soft values are what really drive organizations. When one works with purity of motive, he is working for the best interests of the organization and has common objectives without a hidden agenda. The innovation leader deals with all people in a trustworthy and honest manner, keeping everyone focused and working together.

A good example is found in Chaparral Steel, a small (930 employees) steel mill near Dallas. Here, management trusts employees at all levels. Production workers are taken on sales calls, employees take part in setting their own hours, and there is cross training of jobs and functions. There is an absence of the "we" and "they" attitude among different parts of the operation.[49] Management has extended this attitude by encouraging employees to use their minds in whatever work they are doing. The term "mentofacturing" was coined and is used instead of "manufacturing" to illustrate that all workers are expected to use their mental as well as manual skills as part of doing their best. People generally want to do the right thing. Innovation leaders exhibit and expect the best of motives and people respond accordingly.

Spirit

Spirit is the life force within an organization. It is the feeling you get when you walk into a place, the culmination of all the conscious and unconscious actions. Sometimes you can walk into an environment and feel the positive energy. The spirit pervades the place. There is a hum of positive energy. The innovation leader who radiates that spirited life force encourages enthusiasm and a positive outlook. That contributes to a creative environment, in which ideas flow freely.

During hiring interviews, prospective employees at Southwest Airlines are asked to respond to the following: "Tell me how you recently used your sense of humor in a work environment, and how you have used humor to defuse a difficult situation."[50] At a time when most airlines were downsizing and going through grave financial problems, Southwest Airlines' fortunes soared on the wings of spirit, hard work, and good humor. One employee said, "We take what we do seriously, but we know how to have a good time." Herb Kelleher (1931-), Southwest Airlines' unorthodox CEO and co-founder, told CBS's *60 Minutes*, "It's very simple. I love them. They kid me; they're irreverent toward me. They're a joy to be with. It's a kind of reciprocation there. They know

---

[49] R. Levering, op. cit., pp. 61-63.

[50] Ibid., p. 412.

that I love them and I'm proud of them. When there is a lack of spirit, work becomes tedious, productivity is down, and creativity suffers. Innovation flourishes in a highly spirited atmosphere."

Open-Mindedness

Although Polaroid went through serious marketing problems in the 1980s, it did not compromise its core values.[51] These values include two basic items: creating and selling products that are genuinely unique and useful, and building a worthwhile working life for each member of the company. The respect for employees' opinions and long-term commitment are illustrated in the story of Barbara Waterman. After she was hired as a clerk in 1967, she marched into the office of Tom Wyman, then president, and berated him about racism in the company. "I thought I would be fired," she said. Instead, he talked with her for 25 minutes and finally told her that she should be doing something about this situation at Polaroid. That's when she was assigned to affirmative action, where she is still trying, as she put it, "to get my 40 acres and a mule."

Camaraderie

Camaraderie includes being eager to work with others and hearing what they have to say. It contributes to trust, effective working relationships, and a company's viability. The innovation leader sets the tone for the relationships among people from all the departments with which she works. There is camaraderie at Lands' End, in Dodgeville, Wisconsin.[52] "From time to time, people bring in home-baked cakes and vegetables grown on their farms. And when a snowstorm hits,

---

[51]   Ibid., p. 364.

[52]   Ibid., pp. 232-233.

they really pull together. A four-wheel-drive truck will pick people up at certain points, but sometimes employees are snowed in and can't leave the office—and they talk about those experiences as some of the best they had here," says Richard Anderson (1924-), CEO of Lands' End. He summed up the company philosophy by saying; "I think the first principle of the company, the foundation, is to create an environment for our people in which they are all treated as we would [like to be treated] ourselves."

Humility

Humility carries with it connotations that may seem contradictory to the positive characteristic for innovation. Words such as humiliation, humbling, and the expression "eating humble pie" all emphasize an interpretation of humility that masks its power and strength. Humility has nothing to do with being a doormat for others to walk on. It has everything to do with understanding your place in the scheme of things and being able to use your talent and abilities, without self-aggrandizement, for the benefit of the whole.

Humility is critical for the innovation leader. It allows one to examine and to understand one's own strengths and weaknesses. To truly understand your strengths is not arrogance, and to truly examine your weaknesses is not "putting yourself down." It is another step in creating wisdom by knowing what you do well and what you do not do well.

Federal Express has a policy described by Sorts Systems Manager, Ahmad Jafrey.[53] He sees his management role as a tool to accomplish objectives. "The manager works for the employees. The employee doesn't work for the manager. I don't want authority, I want a job to get done." He would say to the people he supervises, "I don't care how you do it, just do it."

---

[53]   Ibid., p. 123.

Patience and Long-Suffering

Patience and long-suffering is grace under stress. It allows for the natural growth process, which enhances performance. After being at Kodak for about eight years, I was in the company cafeteria complaining to Paul, a senior research scientist, that I had never gotten the opportunity to head a project. I had seen projects fail that I felt I could have seen through, but it seemed nobody would listen to me. Paul looked up and asked how long I had been with the company. When I told him, he said it takes ten years before you will be put in charge of a project. This was not a company policy, Paul explained; it was just his observation over the years. He had been around a long time, and that seemed to be the way it worked. Of course I was angry, since I "knew" I was well suited to run a particular project and my management was making a mistake by not giving me the opportunity. Paul gave me perspective. I realized that my problem was accepting cultural reality.

Patience is something that I did not learn easily, but since that conversation with Paul in the cafeteria many years ago, I have grown to appreciate its importance. There are things that cannot be rushed; there are time frames that are beyond control. I have also learned that things always seem to take longer than you plan for or expect.

Service

Service means meeting the needs of others. It has to do with doing the right thing under the appropriate circumstances.

In the 1980s, John Deere and other farm equipment companies suffered severe setbacks as the bottom fell out of the farm-equipment industry. John Deere survived because it displayed a three-way attitude toward service: to the company itself, to the communities where they were located, and to their customers. The spirit of service was direct, from the company to the customer. "Ray Sprouse, Jr.[54] has been working on the assembly line . . . for nearly 30 years . . . . He told a story about a defective combine that had been shipped to Minnesota. The company sent Sprouse to check into the problem. He recalls: 'I went into the dealership up there, and the people were totally astounded that somebody from the assembly line was there to help them.' Letting an assembly-line worker deal directly with customers was simply unimaginable."

SOFT VALUES THAT DO NOT WORK

Negative characteristics must also be considered or they will tear apart the fabric of the culture of an organization. Not every workplace is noted for the positive elements mentioned earlier. When negative attitudes predominate, the work environment becomes unpleasant, innovation is undermined, and the viability of the company is threatened. It is easier to destroy than to create. Discord can ravage an organization quickly while the positive characteristics are built over time.

Contentiousness

Contention is not to be confused with creative disagreement or active engagement. Under the proper conditions, the clash of differing opinions creates sparks of truth. However, finding and using its value hinges on clearly stating difference before positions get entrenched, and without being possessive of ideas, taking the difference personally, or being disagreeable. Healthy disputes and mind-expanding give-and-take are beneficial. Contentiousness is different. It is counterproductive and should be eliminated. It may also be masking other, more serious problems.

---

[54]   Ibid., p. 95.

Stubbornness

The difference between a stubborn and a resolute person depends on whether or not you agree with her. In reality, it is a matter of motivation. Great achievements have been made because people would not give up. That is persistence. Being stubborn is being unreasonably obstinate, always insisting on your own way, and being unable to admit the value of other viewpoints. Stubbornness guarantees discord and wrangling, and inhibits innovation. When faced with stubbornness, it often helps to get the individuals involved to see the larger picture.

Pride

Ideas are something like children: your own are wonderful. Like children, they must be given the freedom to become whatever they can be. If someone has an idea and hangs on to it so tightly that he cannot see different perspectives or will not consider modifications, that idea will not have the room it needs to grow and develop. Innovation is usually more dependent on how an idea develops than on its original form; therefore, collaboration and cooperation are essential for the innovation process to work. There is nothing wrong with gaining satisfaction from something done well, but leave it alone. Don't dwell on it or it will never get improved.

Discounting

Constructive criticism is of great value, but belittling the contributions of others or putting down their ideas saps energy and impedes innovation. It erodes feelings of trust and teamwork. George Prince (1918-) at Synectics has concluded that the put-down is the greatest enemy to creativity.[55] Many

---

[55]   W. J. Gordon, *Synectics: The Development of Creative Capacity*, Harper and Row, New York, 1961.

people find it hard to come forward with contributions if they or their ideas are thought to be of little value.

A company started an innovation system to solicit new business and/or technology from its employees. When ideas came in, the manager who ran the process put the papers describing the ideas in a drawer. Once a month, division managers would meet to review the ideas. They asked me to come to one of their meetings to observe their process. Copies would be made and distributed; the originator would be called in to explain the idea and interrogations would begin. Some of the managers did not want to be part of the process and their boredom and inattention was obvious. Others seemed intent on finding reasons to kill the ideas. Flaws would be pointed out and the originator would be told to get more information or improve this or that. Then, the originator would be dismissed. When the session was over, the proposals were put back in the drawer to await the next meeting. There was nothing positive about the meeting, which was really a discounting session. The result was that few of the originators bothered to return, and the number of ideas submitted declined sharply. The managers concluded that the employees did not have any worthwhile ideas. Had they made the meetings positive and supportive rather than negative, they would have experienced an increase in the number of ideas submitted. The company missed out on some potentially valuable ideas because the managers did not know how to handle either the originators or the ideas they submitted.

Indiscriminate Criticism

Indiscriminate criticism of the organization, its policies, and fellow employees undermines trust, threatens organizational viability, and discourages innovation. Using a searching and critical eye is essential in the pursuit of truth and for effective innovation. Complaining and dwelling on the negative aspects of the organization, or of life in general, interferes with objectivity and undermines the process of innovation. Innovation thrives on hope and optimism. Indiscriminate criticism breeds negativity, despair, pessimism, and failure, and thwarts initiative.

Dominating Attitude

Supervision should never be confused with domination. A friend of mine who is a supervisor at a government facility was asked how many people worked under her. She responded, "No one. There are 42 people whom I supervise and for whom I have responsibility. They work with me—neither under me nor for me!" Hers was a well functioning department.

Managing the Soft Values

Employees are influenced by the soft values, which are the sum of both the positive and negative elements that exist in a company's culture and influence workers. These shared values are the basis for building the networks and trust relationships that are so vital to sustaining innovation.[56]

People displaying negative characteristics may be projecting their fear of job loss, or making the "wrong" decision. They may be afraid of losing power, or afraid that they are aligned with the "wrong people." Sometimes people are afraid that somehow they will be "found out," that a shortcoming they have will be exposed and they will be held up for ridicule or worse. The innovation leader knows and accepts her strengths and weaknesses to coach people through their fears. This frees and enlivens the innovation process.

With healthy and positive soft values, the environment is a place of trust. And, trust is the means that allows innovation to potentially become everyone's job. While trust is the means, love is the unspoken word that holds the system together.

---

[56] See Francis Fukuyama, *Trust: The Social Virtues and the Creation of Prosperity*, The Free Press, New York, 1995.

CHAPTER 9

Trust Is The Means And
Love The Unspoken Word

It is impossible to go through life without trust: that is to be imprisoned in the worst cell of all, oneself.

—Graham Greene (1904-1991), British novelist.

Obstacles, problems, doubts, and objections are frictions that slow down, and can even stop the innovative process. Trust is the means that enables it to glide over friction. Together with love, that unspoken word in the business world, and an explicit covenant, innovations have their best chance for a smooth journey. These are discussed as they relate to working relationships.

Trust has always been essential for earning a living—even when earning a living was hunting for food and when the business unit was the tribal family. The only way early man could hunt the woolly mammoth was by working together with complete trust. In later times, people who trusted one another banned together and made fortifications to protect against those whom they feared or could not trust. One indication that our society is still based on trust is that fraud, embezzlement, and deceit are still news. Trust remains the standard.

Many partnerships have been formed, few work out. Why? There are many reasons. People may start with common objectives, but objectives change over time and if the partners no longer have common dreams, a rift occurs. As work progresses, envy or jealousy may develop and egos get in the way. If talents, skill, and activities are competitive instead of complementary, there is little chance for success. The first thing to go is trust, then friction reigns and the enterprise comes to a halt.

Covenantal Relationships

The highest compact we can make with our fellow is—
"Let there be truth between us two forevermore."

—*Ralph Waldo Emerson (1803-1882),*
American writer and philosopher.

There is no end to the variety of working agreements between companies and their employees or between managers and the people who report to them. The most meaningful and productive relationships involve more than simple agreements or contracts: they are covenants. Why speak of a covenant? The word connotes a solemn bond with the strength of an oath and presence of emotional commitment. Having a clear covenant is a principle for sustaining innovation because innovations flourish when relationships are based on a commitment that goes beyond agreements or contracts. In a legal sense, it denotes a formal agreement, especially one under seal. In real estate, it refers to special conditions regulating property use. In a religious sense, it is a conditional promise made to humanity by God. Between two people, it is a solemn, unbreakable pledge.

A highly respected coworker once told me something that summarizes the essence of that relationship. "When you work for someone who pays you and you take the money, you owe him more than a day's work for a day's wages. You owe him your loyalty and support. It is immoral to accept money and then criticize the company or the owner in a negative way. If you are going to talk against the organization, wait until after you are no longer taking its money."

Traditionally, there has been an implicit covenant in the form of an understanding. In many companies, if employees did well by the company, the company would look out for their best interests and take care of them. This was rarely stated, yet was implicit and understood, and accepted by all. The unstated covenant had two parts: 1) the employee was expected to do good work, and 2) the company was expected to provide job security. In short, if people worked hard, the company would take care of them. People who worked for companies such as Kodak, General Electric, IBM, or Ford Motor Company in years past knew they could count on the company and planned their lives around conditions of the unstated covenant.

These covenants were not vague, philosophical ideas; employees **knew** they could stay until retirement. Based on that expectation, people made major purchases, such as buying a house or making plans for their children's education. Sometimes companies would even make low-interest loans available. These covenants kept the expectations and understandings of all people within the organization aligned.

Serious problems develop when there is a discrepancy between what people expect and the objectives of top management, and vice versa. When that happens trust and loyalty are among the first victims. Once, I asked a group of executives how many of them expected to spend their entire career working at their current place of employment. Few of them did. A generation ago, leaving a large, established company was an exception. Today, staying with the organization is the exception.

There are many reasons for this difference, but one significant factor is that employees no longer have the confidence that companies will treat their people fairly. An unspoken covenant used to bond employees to their companies. Employees believed that if they gave their loyalty to their companies, the companies would return that loyalty with job security. That bond has been broken, and it has been a gut-wrenching experience. It takes the heart out of people's sense of security and erodes feelings of loyalty to their companies.

A new covenant needs to be established with certain mutual benefits. The covenant needs to be explicit and clearly understood by all. People should be committed to serving each other, the organization and its customers, and be rewarded accordingly when they become parties to this covenant.

Creating an Explicit Covenant

Creating an explicit covenant is the *right thing to do*. A clear, concise covenant keeps the expectations of all parties aligned. It gives a mutual understanding of the relationship and warrants fair behaviors from both parties. It is the moral high ground. The covenant can be as limited or as broad as the organizational leadership wants it to be.

Furthermore, internal support is needed for *stability* and organizational *viability*. Survival in this highly competitive age is improved when there is a dedicated and loyal work force committed to the success of the company. When people stay with their companies for the long haul, there is *continuity*. Innovations flourish in a *secure setting*. A covenant makes people eager to find new and better ways to help a company prosper and helps create an environment within which creative ideas thrive. Innovation involves risk-taking, and trust is essential to accepting the risks involved with exploring new ventures.

A new covenant could grant qualified people work for life, if that is what they want. Qualification would be based on both employee commitment and competencies. It would also be dependent upon the solvency of the company. There is a major difference between layoffs for survival and layoffs used to enhance the bottom line. Layoffs should be the last line of defense since they tend to be counterproductive.

Downsizing solely for increased profitability is a major violation of the unspoken covenant. Ironically, except for a short-term improvement in stock value, downsizing generally does not improve profitability. In 1996, the International Group of the American Management Association found that fewer than half of the companies that downsized (44 %) found an operational profit the next year. It also reported that 72.2 % of the downsizing companies showed a decline in employee morale and experienced a much higher turnover rate.[57] A separate study completed in 1995 by Deborah Doughty and Edward H. Bowman, reported a reduction in the number of innovations inside the downsized companies.[58] The innovation leader should not be surprised, since innovators depend upon being able to communicate freely with a high degree of trust, and with people in different parts of the organization. Innovators set up informal networks within organizations to accomplish their objectives. Downsizing rips holes in those networks. Even when the most innovative people are retained, they are handicapped because people in their networks, on whom they have come to rely, are no longer with the company. I explained this in a speech in Cleveland and one senior executive in the audience remarked, "That's like cutting holes in your fishing net before you go fishing."

Another problem with downsizing is that when a company lays-off a significant percentage of its work force, everyone

---

[57] *1996 AMA Survey*, "Corporate Downsizing, Job Elimination and Job Creation," Summary of Key Findings.

[58] D. Doughty and E. H. Bowman, "The Effects of Organizational Downsizing on Product Innovation," *California Management Review*, 1995, p. 37.

may feel as if the implicit covenant has been broken. Confidence is severely shaken. Disability claims can rise by as much as 70%.[59] Those who are left wonder how long it will be before they too become victims.

Who will be the first ones to send out résumés and be successful in finding new jobs? The best qualified people, the very ones the company should want to keep. If 10 % of the work force is laid off, including some nonproductive people, there is also going to be an exodus of the most productive ones. If you put a hidden camera by the copying machines, you would see a lot of people making copies of their résumés to mail out with the hope of landing a job elsewhere.

One employee of a major American firm that recently laid-off a large number of employees stated his reaction: "Monday we fired over 100 people out of our 550-person division. I was fine, but I couldn't believe how much it hurt even though I was not personally affected." The decision makers called it "downsizing." But this employee, who lived in the real world, called it by its proper name—"being fired." As of this writing, this highly valued employee is actively seeking employment elsewhere. Another employee of the same firm, whose department was not affected, started a part-time business of his own. He told me, "I'll get this business up and running so that when they start cutting in my department, I'll have somewhere to go."

It is no wonder that the International Group of the American Management Association found a decrease in employee morale in companies that have downsized. Nor is it any wonder that an executive placement firm found that 72 % of the executives they surveyed were seeking new positions. More than 60 % of them had either sent out résumés or been

---

[59]   Martha Peak, "Cutting Jobs? Watch Your Disability Expenses Grow," *Management Review*, March 1997, p. 9.

interviewed for new positions within the past year.[60] These executives may be improving their own career paths, but this is not the way to build stable organizations based on the trust and commitment of a covenant.

Layoffs for survival are another matter. In 1997, Apple Computer cut 31 % of its payroll because the life of the company was at stake.[61] This was well communicated, understood, and, even though employees didn't want to leave, they accepted their situation as a business imperative.

The major thing that is lost with large-scale layoffs is commitment. That extremely important quality is rarely addressed directly even though it is essential to an organization's viability. I have identified four levels of commitment to the organization on the part of people working within that organization. I call them *partners, stewards, employees*, and *contractors*.

These levels of commitment are not dependent on the nature of the work people do, where people are on the organizational chart, how long they have worked for the company, or what kind of contract each may have. Members of each group are found in all departments and in all levels of the organization, whether managerial, shop workers, fulltime, part-time, or temporary. These are categories of commitment, not positions.

To a large extent, the differences among them are related to focus and orientation. One point of focus is on the well-being and success of the organization. In contrast, others may be more focused on their personal agenda, a specific project, or assigned task. Figure 9.1 represents a traditional organizational or power chart as well as an organizational commitment chart.

[60]   *1996 AMA Survey*, op. cit.

[61]   Tom Moore, "Building Credibility in a Time of Change," *Communication World Online*, 1996.

Figure 9.1

Traditional Organizational Chart

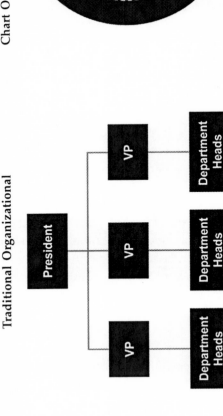

Typical organizational charts reflect hierarchical power relations within organizations and are based on levels of decision-making authority and responsibility.

Organizational Commitment Chart

The commitment chart reflects the relationship between an individual and an organization, based on the degree of personal commitment toward the company. The closer an individual is to the center of the chart, the higher his or her level of commitment. What has always been considered a "higher" job does not bring one automatically to the center of this chart; a senior vice president can act as an "employee," just as a maintenance worker can act as a "steward."

Levels of Commitment

The traditional organizational chart in Figure 9.1 shows who has decision-making authority, who reports to whom, and how the various departments are related to each other. An organizational chart helps everyone understand the decision-making process of the organization.

I have found that traditional tables of organization are unable to reflect the commitment level of the individuals within an organization. So I created the *commitment chart*, which is also depicted in Figure 9.1. It shows the commitment levels as concentric rings. Here, four separate relationships exist within organizations: *partners, stewards, employees,* and *contractors*.

Partners are those who have a strong sense of ownership in the company. Their work gives meaning to their lives; it is part of their identity. The commitment to the wellbeing of the company, its employees, and its customers is strong, and the partner spends a considerable amount of time thinking about the business. The company's and the partner's identity are intertwined.

Stewards feel strongly about the success of the company and, while their identity is not as wrapped up in the company as the partners,' they are apt to spend many extra hours working on company business. There is a strong sense of pride in what they are doing and of the achievements by the organization. Stewards are constant promoters, well-wishers, and defenders of the company, its policies, and its products. A long-time relationship with the company is taken for granted.

Employees do their jobs conscientiously and work hard for the company. On occasion they may do extra work and are supporters of the company. They are not so committed to a long-term relationship with the company as the stewards, and may feel free to leave the organization readily when a more attractive opportunity comes along.

Contractors fulfill their job requirements. They may be highly competent and do excellent work and have a strong sense of commitment. However, their commitment is to the project and/or their profession, not the organization. Their goals may or may not be aligned with those of the organization. Company loyalty is not an important factor.

The traditional power chart and the commitment chart *are not just different views of the same structure*. They both communicate important information that has distinct content, and they are independent of one another.

There are people who are at the partner level on the assembly line, in maintenance, and on the sales force. You will also find the contractor's perspective at the top levels of management. There are behaviors related to commitment, which are represented by the concentric rings. Those closest to the core are most aligned with the objectives and are committed to the well-being of the company; those at the outer rings have the least commitment to the organization. To help understand probable behaviors, think about what people at each commitment level would do if they suddenly received a lot of money, such as a large inheritance or winning a major lottery.

At the core are the *partners*, whose objectives and identity are clearly and strongly aligned with the mission and the vision of the organization. If a *partner* were to come into a lot of money, she would think, "That's great; I don't have to worry about retirement," and go right back to work. The idea of leaving the business, even when financially possible, is not a serious consideration.

If the *steward* were to come into a lot of money, he would think, "Good. Now I can retire earlier." The *steward* does not want to hurt the company and decides to talk to whomever he reports to and plans for a smooth transition. Maybe it will take six months; maybe it will take a year. The person will stay for as long as it takes to make certain that ongoing projects will not be interrupted. There is no desire to create a problem, cause needless worry, or be a burden on anyone in the organization.

When an *employee* wins the lottery, she says, "This is great; I can retire now." She tells the supervisor, "I'm ready to retire. Who do you want me to deliver my work to? Do you want me to stay on for another two weeks or four weeks?" There is a party and everyone has a great time, and the *employee* is on her way.

When the *contractor* gets the money, as soon as the current project is finished, he disappears and may never be seen again.

All four levels are found in every large organization. All play important roles. However, the more partners and stewards there are, the greater the prospects for a long, stable continuation of the business.

Don Braun was in charge of facilities and distribution at Idea Connections. We entertain many guests, and in doing that we usually have a fruit bowl, coffee, and tea served on a buffet, and sometimes have pastries or some other treat available depending on the time of day. Supplying these refreshments was part of Don's responsibility. An important guest was scheduled to meet with me in the office over the weekend. I could handle refreshments, so there was no reason for Don to commute on his day off. I hadn't even told Don that we had a guest coming. When I arrived to prepare for our guest's arrival, I found everything set up—including a tray of bagels. Don had seen the meeting on my calendar and without being asked, had come in early, prepared the refreshments, and left to ensure our guest was well received.

What kind of people do you want working within your company? Do you want people who feel a loyalty for the organization, who share the dream and are committed to the company's mission and vision? Or, would you rather have someone who is looking for a new job? I own a company. I want people working within my organization who are in for the long haul. I want to have people who are committed to the company's success.

There is also a problem of misalignment in perceptions of commitment. An employee may see himself as a steward where his supervisor may see him as a contractor. It helps to have all employees place themselves on the commitment chart and discuss how they understand it. This discussion goes far toward building understanding and trust.

Specific behaviors are associated with each level, as indicated on the following commitment chart (see Figure 9.2).

Figure 9.2: Commitment Behaviors Chart

	Contractor	Employee	Steward	Partner
I vs. We Orientation	"I did this"	"We did this"	"We did this"	"We did this"
What's Protected	Protects career options	Protects job	Protects the stability of the business	Protects the existence and growth of the business
Allegiances	Individual/ Professional	Profession and people inside company	Company and its people	Company's survival, growth, and its people
Standards for Excellence	Professional expertise	Defined by job	Defined by the business and its growth and stability	Defined by business success, growth, and stability
Expectations	Expects respect	Expects the company to behave responsibly toward them	Expects responsibility from self and others	Expects loyalty from self and others
Basis for Personal Identity	Profession	Company role	Position and its responsibility to company	The company
People vs. Business Orientation	Self-orientation	Employee before the company	The company before the employee	The company before the employee
Willingness to Sacrifice	Sacrifices for self-development. Compensation is primary. Expects market pay.	Sacrifices to meet job requirements. Compensation is important. Expects market pay.	Sacrifices what is necessary to do the job. Compensation is important.	Sacrifices everything for the business. Compensation is important.
Domaine of Responsibility	Responsibility taken according to compensation	Responsible for performing job requirements	Fully responsible for their domaine of the business	Feels responsible for everything about the business
Time Commitment	Works by the clock	Works by the clock with some flexibility	Does what's necessary regardless of the clock	Not concerned about time spent. Does the "right thing"

Expected models of behavior are described for the different levels of commitment

The level of commitment is a key factor in maintaining healthy soft values and the importance of service. When everyone understands and accepts the same elements of the covenant, there is alignment. The higher the standard, the more effective the organization and the better the needs will be fulfilled. Misalignment occurs when employees are led to believe one thing and management moves in a different direction.

In the past, when senior executives were promoted from within the company, they were usually people who put their heart, soul, and sweat into the success of the organization. Their dreams were closely aligned with the objectives of the company, and the continued success of the organization was their primary concern. They had an intuitive sense of the unspoken covenant.

In too many companies today, top management and the boards of directors have a contractor's mentality, or to use the sports analogy from Chapter 8, they are so focused on the scoreboard of profitability that they have lost sight of the field of play. Some are so focused on their own career advancement or financial standing that decisions are self-serving rather than committed to the best interests of the organization. Some CEOs, known as hired guns, deliberately pursue short-term gain, even though it may cause long-term injury to the company.

New leadership brought in from outside sources can have great value, especially when it also brings fresh thinking that can find new solutions to old problems. When Robert Townsend (1920-1998) took over as CEO of the financially troubled Avis Rent A Car System, Inc., he made an agreement with Andre Meyer—who had hired him—that neither of them would mention the value of Avis stock for two years.[62] He knew that the changes being made for the survival of the company would create short-term financial confusion and drive down stock value. His goal was to save the company while maintaining the best interests of the stockholders,

---

[62] Robert Townsend, *Up the Organization*, Alfred A Knopf, Inc., New York, 1970, p. 68.

employees, and the customers. He did not focus on maximum, immediate returns for investors or special privileges for top management. He negotiated down his own starting salary, and a year later, when the board wanted to give him a raise, he argued that as CEO he should not get a raise when the company was not yet showing a profit.[63] As a result of his efforts, the company went from the brink of bankruptcy to financial success and stability.

Working Relationships

A healthy working relationship is a stimulus for fostering innovation. This can be accomplished by building trust through three special working relationships: *reciprocity, cooperation*, and *mutual aid*.

Reciprocity is doing something for each other in exchange for like consideration—the working application of "You scratch my back and I'll scratch yours." Within an organization, it can be as simple as employees exchanging days off or covering for one another during an unexpected interruption, knowing that the favor will be returned as needed.

Like individuals, organizations form working relationships built upon the value they can provide to one another. Trust comes from a history of performance and is often more important than price. Among companies, it includes an understanding for the use of each other's goods and services. Innovators network the same way. There is generally a history of people exchanging favors with one another on an informal basis. This is in addition to the duties described by their job descriptions. Someone asks for a favor and you do it. Someday, you might ask that person for a favor in return and you know that, if possible, it will be honored. There are, of course, some people who take but don't return. There are others who remember everything they have done for someone else and

---

[63]   Ibid., p 152.

forget what others have done for them. These people sooner or later are dropped out of networking loops.

A friend in an office where I worked was complaining because one of the secretaries was not giving his work the priority attention she once had given it. I asked him what he had done for her lately. At first he didn't understand the question, and said, "What do you mean?" I said, "Look, you have asked her to do a lot of things for you and she has done them. But, what have you done for her? It looks to me as if this has been a one-way street. Is that fair?" He stopped taking her for granted, started doing little things for her, and was amazed at how well she responded.

Formal records are never kept, but people unconsciously keep track of who owes what to whom. It is normal, natural, healthy and a highly effective reciprocity. It is the way things work in barter societies. There is a Russian saying about obtaining goods and services: "It is better to have 100 friends than 100 Rubles."

Cooperation is working together for a common objective, directly in parallel functions or independently toward a common goal. Its invisible foundation is reciprocity; the success of any form of cooperation requires trust. Cooperation often involves work in teams, either formal or informal, either in tandem or in relay. All activities are based on a confidence that other members are contributing their share. Teams vary. There are coordinated teams, such as in American football, where each player has an assigned role to be carried out with specialized expertise. In an interactive team, such as a jazz ensemble, there is an intricate interplay and shifting of roles. Both forms work well in specific situations, even though their natures are strikingly different.[64]

Mutual aid involves coming to someone's assistance as needed without the expectation of a returned favor. It may include both reciprocity and cooperation, but it is not based on

---

[64] For further discussion, see Jon R. Katzenbach and Douglas K. Smith, *The Wisdom of Teams*, Harper Business Books, New York, 1994.

either one of them. It is an aspect of altruism. There is no sense of "what's in it for me?" but there is a deep, unspoken conviction that others would do likewise if the situation were reversed.

Harvest season in the grain fields of the Midwest has long been a time of intense hard work. Annual income is dependent upon a successful harvest. A wheat farmer I know was in a near-fatal accident at the beginning of the harvest season. He was in the hospital for an extended period of time, unable to tend to the duties of harvest. His neighbors picked a day, brought their own equipment and hired help to his fields, and harvested his crop while he was incapacitated. Not one of those neighbors thought in terms of the favor being returned. They did it because he was a neighbor in need.

A woman in our company was losing her hair during chemotherapy. She used good humor during her ordeal and would wear funny hats—mainly baseball caps. Some of the other employees got together and made arrangements for her to have a fitting at an exclusive hat shop and get an elegant, custom-made hat. She not only got a beautiful hat, but that gesture did wonders for her morale as well as the morale of all those who were involved. Relating this incident to someone who did not work there, she said, "What a wonderful place to work!"

The strength of these working relationships does not show up on the balance sheet, but they form the core of the culture and are the building blocks of organizational trust. Healthy, trusting relationships make people want to work for an organization and do their best.

The importance of managing and creating a covenant cannot be overstated. Establishing an explicit covenant allows everyone involved to understand the ground rules that build trust; it is essential for partners and stewards to have a clear understanding of their mutual commitment. The covenant, whether implied or explicit, has a profound effect on innovation, as trust is a keystone of the process.

The following two charts (see Figure 9.3) illustrate a spectrum of relationships between people (not to the organization).

Figure 9.3:
Relationship Spectrum Between Two Individuals

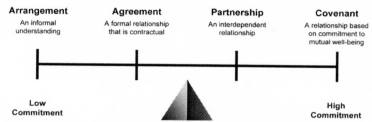

This shows a scale of working relationships between two people. The commitment to the relationship increases as one moves to the right.

This scale may be a useful tool to help identify where one's relationship currently fits and where the relationship should be; it can also identify the level of commitment that is required to successfully conduct business.

Figure 9.4:
Defining Elements of the Relationship Spectrum

Relationship Elements	Relationship Elements	Arrangement An informal understanding	Agreement A formal relationship that is contractual	Partnership An interdependent relationship	Covenant A relationship based on commitment to mutual well-being
Observable Characteristics	Contribution	Variable	Contractual	Going the extra mile	For well-being
	Responsibility	Low	Obligatory	Shared & reciprocal	Absolute
	Approach to the task	Mixed	As defined by the agreement	Consultative	As a steward for the individual and org.
	Source of intimacy	Minimal	Professional	Professional and personal	Personal & emotional (spiritual)
	Commitment to the individual	Little	Bound by the agreement	Strong through the partnership	All-encompassing
"Invisible" Behavioral Drivers	Trust	Minimal	Bonded	High and explicit	Total and implicit
	Difference	Limited acceptance	Conditional tolerance	Affirmation of difference	Celebrate and leverage
	Belonging	Little	As defined by the agreement	As agreed to by partners	Beyond self
Outcome & Result	Consequences of violating relationship	Mild discomfort	Loss of business	Separation of the relationship	Sense of abandonment
	Nature of value produced	Minimal	Achievement	Achievement & personal	Personal & emotional (spiritual)
	Organizational outcome	Task	Results	Excellence	Innovation

Behavior characteristics of the relationship spectrum are needed to assess where two individuals fall on the spectrum.

When the appropriate relationship has been identified, the chart in Figure 9.4 can help clarify the behaviors needed to sustain the relationship or to determine what behaviors are needed to reach a higher commitment level. It should clarify how to work toward partnerships and covenantal relationships. Where there are strong bonds of trust, the goal is to move toward a covenantal relationship.

Love in the Workplace

If you can once engage people's . . . love . . . on your side,
you need not fear what their reason can do against you.

—Lord Chesterfield (1694-1773), English statesman.

In a 1957 speech called "Loving Your Enemies," the Reverend Martin Luther King explained that in the Greek language, there are three separate words for love. All of these loves, he said, are "beautiful." The first is *eros*, an aesthetic, romantic, erotic love. The second is *philia*, an affection between intimate friends. The third is *agape*. This love, he says, "is something of the understanding, creative, redemptive goodwill for all men that seeks nothing in return." For King, "It is an overflowing love; it's what theologians would call the love of God working in the lives of men."[65]

Inside the lives of men and women, in their places of work and rest, this love can transform hearts and minds, and gatherings and collectives of men and women. There is nothing trivial about this love; it is as potent a social force as there can be. And yet, for various reasons, business people shy away from the word. To them, love implies fuzzy thinking, weakness, and "feel good" management. Some people think it is antithetical to reason or to make the tough decisions required in business.

---

[65] Martin Luther King, Jr., public domain sermon, delivered at Dexter Avenue Baptist Church, Montgomery, Alabama, November 17, 1957.

It is as if feeling and thinking were opposites or mutually exclusive. At another deeply human level, perhaps no one wants to risk placing such an important word in a context that is so often more about personal gain than about transforming the world. I feel very strongly that love defines how people should treat one another, and how they can transform their environments.

The idea of love, therefore, has everything to do with creating healthy, thriving businesses and sustaining innovation. Most successful business people have a deep and profound love for what they are doing. That emotion motivates them to take risks and put forth extraordinary energy. While they might not call it love, many entrepreneurs stay with their businesses long after they could comfortably retire. What, other than love of what they are doing, could induce them to stay at their work when it is no longer necessary? They have a deep love for something. It may be their company, making money, or a love for what they are creating.

In her thought-provoking book, *Managing with the Wisdom of Love*,[66] Dorothy Marcic demonstrates the bottom-line value of managing with love. She gives many concrete examples where love within the organization has had a definite and positive impact on bottom-line results. Starting at the top of the organization, when genuine love is demonstrated, a culture is created that is marked by trust, commitment, and mutual respect. The affairs of the organization are well ordered, and its views, position, and reputation are well established and honored. Executives and innovation leaders who are concerned about the viability of their companies should love their people because the people are the company.

But, what does it mean to love your people? What does genuine love look like in the workplace? It means caring for others and being concerned about their personal and professional well-being. It means being consistent in placing a high value on their interests. It means listening and trying to understand their

---

[66]   See *Managing with the Wisdom of Love, op. cit.*

concerns. It means respecting their intelligence and giving credit to their ideas and contributions to the organization.

Genuine love is the ultimate manifestation of trust.

There are some companies, called heritage companies, that are mainly privately owned, often by a family. Some have existed for generations and are based on a foundation of love for the employees. One example is Malden Mills in Lawrence, Massachusetts, which was founded in 1906 by the grandfather of Aaron Feuerstein, the current owner.

Malden Mills was a $400 million firm that employed 2,400 people in its nine-building plant.[67] It was best known for its synthetic sheepskin called Polar Fleece. The business was well run, had plenty of work, and was operating 24 hours a day. On the night of December 11, 1995, while Feuerstein was away celebrating his 70th birthday, a fire raced through the compound and destroyed all nine buildings. Fortunately, no one was injured.

When Feuerstein returned, smoldering embers were all that was left of the business that had been his life. He did have choices. He could collect the insurance money and retire, which is what his financial advisors said he should do; he could move his business to a country with a lower standard of living and cheaper labor costs; or he could rebuild.

His people had seen their very livelihoods go up in smoke. The Christmas holidays were approaching and they did not know what would happen next. They were anxious to hear what Feuerstein had to say. The first thing he did was to announce that all full-time and hourly employees would continue to be paid through the holidays. He even paid the promised holiday bonus of $275 to each employee. Then, he decided to rebuild. His people were paid during the rebuilding and were involved with planning the new facility. The factory was rebuilt under budget and in less time than was expected.

---

[67] "Courage in the Workplace," and "After the Fire at Malden Mills," *The Work Doctor*, Benicia, California, 1996.

To Feuerstein, the decision to stay and rebuild was not only the smart choice for his business, it was the right thing to do. On television, he said, "Why am I doing this? I consider the employees the most valuable asset Malden Mills has. I don't consider them, like some companies do, as an expense that can be cut. I know in the long run that what I'm doing will come back tenfold and will make Malden Mills the best company in the industry."[68] He didn't talk about how the action would benefit him, but what the results would be for his people and his company.

Love is also demonstrated in publicly held companies. Southwest Airlines is a good example. In *The 100 Best Companies to Work for in America*, the following is stated about Southwest Airlines. "The Southwest family talks a lot about love. Some of it seems hokey to an outsider, such as their employee magazine being called *Luv Lines* (with a dot over the "i" in the shape of a heart). During their 20th anniversary in 1991, the company's slogan, appearing on stationery and in ads, was '20 Years of Loving You.' Their New York Stock Exchange ticker symbol is LUV. And Southwest's flight attendants serve 'love potions' (drinks) and 'love bites' (peanuts)."[69]

In Chapter 7, CEO Herb Kelleher was quoted on *60 Minutes* as saying about his employees, "It's very simple. I love them."[70] This feeling is reciprocated. "There seems to be a genuine sense of affection among employees, toward each other and their larger-than-life CEO. As Chuck Martin says: 'Herb Kelleher is Southwest Airlines. We all love him.'

Managing in an Environment of Trust

There is a long-standing interest in the importance of different people within an organization. Nearly two thousand years ago, the

---

[68]   Ibid. Also cited in "Malden Mills: What a Great Place to Work..." in *National Association of Working People*, volume 1, issue no. 1, August 1996

[69]   Levering and Moskowitz, op. cit., p. 413.

[70]   Ibid., p. 416.

Apostle Paul, in his first letter to the Corinthians, listed the members of the congregation in order of importance. At the bottom of the list, and therefore the least important, was "government." In industry today, that would be the managers. This is a profound and sobering perspective. Paul put them at the bottom rather than the top in importance. Without the workers, managers are superfluous. And, without trust between them, friction is guaranteed.

When looking at people to fill management positions I look for six standards. Two are commitment qualities, three relate to competencies, and the final one is the ability to integrate the first five.

Commitment qualities:

- **Unquestioned loyalty:** Supporting the company and being its defender and ambassador of goodwill. When problems arise, it means taking appropriate corrective action rather than complaining or finding fault.
- **Steadfast devotion:** This is going beyond minimum expectations. It means deep and sustained concern for the best interests of the organization and making certain it is well served. It involves putting forth the necessary effort to be sure things are done properly.

People who demonstrate these levels of commitment are the ones who are going to make sure the company is well served and will remain viable. Commitment, however, is not enough. People must also demonstrate competencies.

Competencies:

- **A well-trained mind.** People need a solid understanding of their professional role, seeking to expand their knowledge and improve their understanding of the job. They continue to develop their problem-solving skills and clear thinking.

- **Recognized ability.** Paper credentials are not enough. The way in which a person is viewed by her peers, subordinates, supervisors, and customers is often the clearest measure of ability.
- **Mature experience.** As skill and ability are applied in the workday world, people mature and improve. Experience tempers skill and ability, and renders them increasingly useful.

Ability to integrate

Those who best combine the above qualities of commitment and competence are the stewards and the partners who best serve the organization. They can be trusted, they are balanced, and *they are the bedrock of all organizations and are the people I want working with me.*

In dealing with peers and subordinates, the innovation leader follows the principles of a covenant. Without promising to accomplish everything, he lets it be known that he will do everything within reason on their behalf. Marty was working for a toy company that used the services of several contractors. He knew that many firms delayed or manipulated payments to contractors. He didn't think that was fair, and made sure that the contractors he worked with were paid as soon as their work was delivered. Without informing Marty, the senior management at the toy company made a policy change. Henceforth, all contractors would be paid by mail. Marty learned of this when a contractor submitted his bill and was refused his check. Marty was furious. He went directly to the president of the company and said, "You just fired me." The president didn't understand, so Marty explained, "Look, I told these people that they will get paid as soon as they turn in their work. That is a promise. It's like a covenant. If I can't get a check for this man today, this is not a place where I want to work. So, if you don't pay him, you are firing me." A check was made out immediately.

Clever slogans by themselves are inadequate. Trust is demonstrated by the day-to-day, personal dealings. It is at the basis of the culture of a vital and vibrant organization. It permeates all dealings. There is no substitute for it. For the innovation leader, working under a covenant means being willing to put yourself on the line as Marty did. It is part of the covenant established with the people with whom you work. There are many ways to build trust. I know of a leader whose favorite "sport" seems to be doing nice things for others anonymously. In fact, he gets a sheepish look of embarrassment whenever he is caught in one of his many acts of anonymous kindness. Another way is to encourage and applaud acts of mutual aid that spontaneously occur among workers. Simple gestures, like celebrating victories together, are also an excellent way to build the camaraderie and trust that make working relationships fun and effective.

Hotels are noted for having many jobs at the minimum-wage level. Often, these jobs are done by recent immigrants who have common ethnic origins. The workplace often becomes a close-knit enclave. In one large hotel, when the mother of one of the workers in the laundry died, the hotel manager decided to close down the laundry so that all the workers could attend the funeral. It was a great inconvenience for the operation of the hotel, but the manager felt the gesture of love outweighed the business difficulties it caused. The man whose mother had died said, "I will never work anywhere else."

Because trust is the means that allows people in organizations to work together and sustain innovation, and because trust is almost always implied rather than explicit, many organizations assume it is there and do not actively create it or sustain it. Innovation and organization leaders are the ones to introduce the principle of trust consciously and proactively. Understanding the elements that lead to trust makes it possible to make them explicit!

Now that we have discussed the People Principles of sustaining innovation, it is time to see how they fit together.

CHAPTER 10

Putting It All Together

. . . It is first to know and then to do.

—*'Abdu'l-Bahá 'Abbas, Persian Sage (1844-1921).*

The place of the innovation leader in business

Innovation is the most political aspect of the corporate world. To create anything new is a powerful act that gains prestige for the people involved. The more they create, the more powerful innovators become. This can be an enormous threat to those who are not producing new things at the same rate; they feel their power and authority eroding when an idea that is not theirs or that is not under their control succeeds. Therefore, these people become overly protective of the areas over which they do have control—their budgets, spheres of influence, and other resources. This is usually an unconscious act rather than a deliberate effort to undermine, but conscious or unconscious, the intent is to stop anything perceived as a threat to one's authority, position, or personal ambition. As a consequence, lip service will be paid to the need to innovate while doing everything in one's power to stop the results and activities around other people's innovations.

The innovation leader needs to be aware of this political reality and be prepared to protect both the innovation process and the innovators. The most common reason given to stop innovation is that the project does not make good business sense and, in most cases, this justification may be sincerely believed. But too often, an innovation threatens personal and/ or business agendas. The innovation leader can become the first victim of jealous, political intrigue unless ideas and their creators are managed with care.

Michelangelo saw beauty within the marble, and chipped at the marble to free the spirit, the beauty trapped within. In that same sense, the innovation leader is an artist who releases the innovative potential of an organization by chipping away at whatever holds innovation back.

There's an old saying, "You can't push the river." A river can, however, be directed. Canals are built and dams constructed, but these use, rather than oppose, the energy of the river. The innovation leader can help affect change, and direct the flow of the river, but the success of any project will require *knowledge, volition,* and *action.*

> **Knowledge**—Knowledge is the foundation upon which everything is built. First, you need to know what to do. That is why it is important to have a profound understanding and appreciation of what is to be accomplished, and the principles that can bring about the desired results.

> **Volition**—After you've understood the nature of a task and the principles that apply to it, the will to act is required. Do you have the volition to lead innovation and the passion it takes to make it happen?

> **Action**—Without action, all the aforementioned is
> of little value. Ventures, like rivers, create energy.
> By working with the flow of the river, and using its
> inherent energy, you can use it to advantage.
> Sustained innovation makes use of the energy
> created by the process. That is accomplished when
> you operate on the level of principle.

Innovation leaders must know and understand problems, have the desire to work problems out, and must seize the day. They must be guided by principles. In their dealings with passionate innovators and corporate managers, they have a role that is part accountant, part master artist, part court jester, and part friend. Theirs is an honorable and exciting role— beginning with ideas and ending with infinite possibilities.

*   *   *

This book began with a rather simple idea: that innovation is a *human* process and therefore succeeds or fails depending on a set of *human* principles. I have tried to show how these human principles are more than just the window-dressing on a corporation's neat plan to maximize profits. They are essential to the healthy working of any organization, and to the process of innovation in particular. A suggestion box, brimming with ideas, is of no use if it is ignored. The genius of the innovator will come to naught if the pain that accompanies her passion is not understood. Trust is essential. Without it, the bond between people will disintegrate; so that even the best ideas they generate together will die along with their connection.

In the broad sense, I certainly did not invent the principles presented here; one way or another, most of them come from the great spiritual traditions of the world. The fact that people must be treated with dignity and respect in order to reap the benefits of their diverse talents is a spiritual truism. The fact that we need to think seriously about these principles within the context of growing, changing, flourishing *businesses* is what I have tried to make clear in these pages.

I've run a business for 15 years. I know firsthand that these principles are difficult to apply consciously and consistently. At times, I've learned the hard way that ignoring them, even for a short time, can jeopardize the well-being of my own organization. For years, I've puzzled over these matters, talked them over with friends and colleagues, and slowly sifted down the principles. Ultimately, I've tried my best to live by them. My hope is that this book helps others to do the same.

An organization can be seen as an organic entity. Like any living thing, it requires suitable conditions and nurturing to survive. If it is to fully develop and blossom, it requires careful tending. Innovation feeds organizations. It sustains them. When organizations are treated in accordance with timeless human principles, they reach their full, living potential.

An advantage of being a child is you don't have years of logic saying your dreams won't come true.

Adam's words remind me daily how important it is to find the methods and the means of keeping dreams alive. Nurture the dreamers, support their ideas, be honest with them, and see where that takes you.

Sharing what I have learned has been a response to something deep inside—the desire to release the creative potential of people within organizations. When you understand, live by, and use these simple human principles, you can foster and release the creative potential of the people with whom you work. And when you do, *your* journey has just begun.

EPILOGUE

The Essence of Innovation is its principles. I have a suggestion for you as you embark on your Innovation journey. Below I have listed the eight principles that are addressed in my book. They are:

1. Innovation Starts When People Convert Problems Into Ideas
2. Innovation Needs a System
3. Passion Is the Fuel and Pain Is the Hidden Ingredient
4. Co-Locate for Effective Exchange
5. Leverage Differences
6. The Elements of Destruction Are Present at Creation
7. Soft Values Drive the Organization
8. Trust Is the Means and Love the Unspoken Word

The intertwined eight principles of innovation that lead to the final result can best be understood through an analogy of a fruit and its new plant.

The fruit has two major components: the seed and its surroundings called the pericarp. The seed contains all the genetic code necessary to create the new plant. The pericarp has all the nourishment necessary to sustain the seed until the new plant can grow in rich soil.

A Typical Fruit and Seed

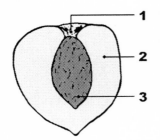

1

2

3

Pericarp: the external part of a fruit.

1. **Exocarp:** the outer covering, or "skin"

2. **Mericarp:** the middle covering or "flesh"

3. **Endocarp:** the inner covering, in many cases the stiffened part known as the "stone"

Seed: The seed is enclosed inside the endocarp

The principles of innovation can also be divided into two groups: the essence and the organizational structure. The first five principles, like seeds, provide the genetic code of the new enterprises. The three organizational principles, like the pericarp, nourish the seed. Both systems can be thought of as an incubator preparing the seed for taking root in supportive soil and the innovation for favorable market conditions.

Some fruits, like a pomegranate, have multiple seeds and some only have one seed. The multiple seed fruit is like a large organization that is able to launch a lot of seeds knowing only a few will survive. The single seed fruit is like a small company that depends heavily on launching one venture. Very few seeds turn into a thriving new growth. The same is true of new undertakings. Few ultimately make it in the market place.

If any necessary condition of either the fruit or the principles of innovation and market conditions are lacking, the new entity will be seriously hampered or not grow at all. The best of seeds need favorable physical conditions to flourish and the best of innovations need favorable market conditions for meaningful success.

Both seeds and innovations contain an additional magic. Any fool can count the number of seeds in an apple. But, who can count the number of apples in a seed? Anyone can see the effects of innovations once they have happened. But, who can count the new ones they will inspire?

Now I would like you to ask yourself this question about your project, "Does what I am about to do contain all the elements associated with each one of these principles which are critical for the success of my innovation project?" Part of your strategy in moving forward should be to embed these principles in your tactical plan.

I have created a workbook, found in Appendix E, containing specific questions that may help you evaluate your usage of each principle.

Please write me at makingtheinvisiblevisible@innovating.com and let me know how you are doing. I wish you much success.

Appendix A

Summary Points

Introduction

- The book is divided into two parts. The first part is the essence of the innovation process. The second part relates to the environment of the innovation process.
- An innovation is a creative act or solution that results in a quantifiable gain (see page 17).
- In the long run, stock prices are generally more closely related to the quality of the work force than to the technology.

Chapter 1—The Human Component In A Changing World.

The human factor is inherent in all the principles for sustaining innovation. Innovation does not happen without people, so managing innovation is managing people.

- A constant flow of new ideas is necessary for any organization to stay healthy. Ideas come from people; there is no other source.

- Three components of sustaining innovation are business, technology, and human. It is the human component that connects the other two and enables them to work together.
- In order to share ideas in a meaningful way, a common vocabulary and understanding of underlying principles is needed. This book was written to begin to provide a common vocabulary and to illuminate the underlying people principles needed to sustain innovation.
- Principles are timeless. Methods and technology change. Sustaining innovation involves applying principles to the circumstances of the moment.

Chapter 2—Innovation Starts When People Convert Problems Into Ideas

Ideas are easy to find. The challenge is to nurture them so they come to fruition. Since we don't know which concepts will succeed, innovation requires many ideas. Ideas can be found in a lot of places, but the greatest—and largely untapped— reservoir of all is in various places within the organization. As more reservoirs are utilized, the organization can better fill the idea pipeline.

- All major developments start as a puzzle or question: a problem from which ideas are generated. This is the beginning of the innovation process.
- Questions are raised in a number of ways, including chance discovery, a significant event, and idle curiosity.
- Innovations sometimes occur incidentally as solutions are being sought for some other problem.
- It frequently takes years, or even centuries, before a nagging question or problem can generate the right idea under the proper circumstance to lead to a quantifiable gain.

- Graham Wallas identified four stages in the creative process: preparation, incubation, illumination, and validation.
- External stimuli, internal stimuli, and group interaction are all sources of ideas.
- While some things are developed by one person working alone, it is more common that many people are involved. Sometimes people work independently of one another. At other times they work as a team. They may work interactively, either parallel or serially, or independently toward a common objective.
- Organizations that lead their industries receive nearly half of their sales from products introduced within the last five years.
- Planned innovations and targeted problems usually produce ideas that are incremental in nature. Most of the significant and breakthrough innovations are unplanned in nature.
- Employees throughout an organization are a reservoir of important ideas, but are usually ignored. Having a system to capture their ideas can provide an important bonus for the company.
- When organizations do not have enough ideas, it is generally because the system has not sufficiently tapped into the idea reservoir available for its use.
- When treated as prized originators-of-ideas, employees will respond with ideas.

Chapter 3—Innovation Needs A System

Ideas integrated into the organization's structure are the ones most apt to produce quantifiable gains. The innovation leader either must have or create a system for innovation to stimulate the flow of innovation. A visible system works better in large organizations; an informal or invisible one works better in smaller organizations. Many options are open. Contributing factors include the environment, the needs of the organization and, above all, a genuine concern for both people and their ideas. The Originator-assisted model, outlined in detail, is one example. Appendix C lists other systems.

- All ideas come from people.
- There are five systems of innovation that can serve to move ideas through an organization: Originator-assisted, Targeted Innovation, Internal Venturing, Continuous Improvement, and Strategic Transfer.
- The Originator-assisted system hasn't received much attention by other authors because it is underused and not well understood. The Office of Innovation at Kodak is an example of an Originator-assisted system. This system, driven by the originators, gives unplanned ideas a "home" and an opportunity to be developed.

  - The process is as follows: idea generation and enhancement; selecting consultants; initial screening; group review, team building and experimentation; seeking champions and sponsorship.
  - An Originator-assisted system is based on having an innovation advocate to facilitate the process. She is successful when she is: centered on people and their ideas; sufficiently experienced and competent technically to understand what the originator hopes to achieve; results oriented; respected and trusted by co-workers throughout the organization; politically astute; aware of why and how an idea fails; and skilled at building and using networks.

- Part of the philosophy of an innovation leader is that ideas can come from people anywhere in the organization.

Chapter 4—Passion Is The Fuel And Pain Is The Hidden Ingredient

It is people of passion who drive ideas to quantifiable gains. Passionate people are often irritating and appear less stable than others; both of these generalizations are frequently true. The innovation leader understands that this irritant in the organization can become useful, like the irritant in an oyster. People who are capable of great passion provide the element needed for the pearl of innovation to be formed. Downsizing an organization usually includes letting go of the people who could produce new pearls. Pain comes with the passion, even though this interrelationship is rarely recognized.

- Passion is necessary to drive innovation and has two ironies. The first is that passion is a gift to the organization; you cannot go out and buy it. The second is that passion scares most managers because it is difficult to control. Terminating the passion stops the innovations.
- The facets of passion include: confidence, energy, tenacity, resilience, focus, response to challenge, and a disregard of criticism.
- People of passion are often people of extremes who are not moved by the things that motivate most other people, such as financial rewards. People of passion tend to be highly independent and unorthodox.
- Passion is not available on command and makes no distinction between ideas that are worthy and those that are doomed to fail.
- With the passion comes pain. Pain not only affects passionate people, but also those around them—family, friends, co-workers, managers, and the organization as a whole. Sometimes the one with the passion does not even feel the pain.
- The innovation leader learns to manage the passion, not the person. This includes: protecting the one with the

passion from the organization, and the organization from the passionate one; reducing the pain and energy needed to overcome obstacles; providing encouragement; focusing attention; and finding a way for passionate and energetic eccentrics to fit within the organization.

Chapter 5—Co-Locate For Effective Exchange

Innovation happens best when collaborators are in close proximity to one another. Trust is built when people co-locate. The fact that modern technology makes it possible for people to operate from remote locations is a temporary and partial extension of co-location; it does not supplant it. Co-location, especially in the early stages of concept development, wards off many otherwise serious problems that would occur. Also, the interaction that is so important to the cross-fertilization and development of ideas would be missed.

- Innumerable subtle and unknown elements of communication are exchanged when people are together physically. Trust and confidence are enhanced when all of the senses are involved.
- Companies should make arrangements so that collaborators are free to make frequent, direct personal contact.
- Co-location is most important at the beginning of a venture.
- There is no substitute for co-location.

Chapter 6—Leverage Differences

People are different. The differences of language, what people hold as important (their currencies), how they think (cognitive differences), ethnic or physio-cultural backgrounds, and gender differences produce major challenges within any organization.

By looking at the differences as valuable assets rather than as problems, it is possible to use the exciting range of human variations for the benefit of all. Every group has something special to contribute to the whole. In order to leverage these contributions, it is first necessary to understand that differences are real, valuable, and important. The next step is to appreciate the intrinsic value of these differences. The final step is to apply the skill of leveraging differences to produce maximum impact on the innovation process. Differences enhance both innovation and the organization by constructively combining complementary capabilities.

- When it is possible to get beyond the problems that the differences among groups create, it is possible to learn that each group has something of value for others.
- Words both inform, by conveying information, and define who is and who is not a member of a particular group. Innovations are facilitated when the innovation leader learns to understand and speak the language of other groups and can properly interpret non-verbal cues.
- Currency is a medium of exchange and establishes relative importance and value. It is not always money. It may be recognition, power, prestige, security, or good feelings. Rewards are best when they incorporate the values of the recipient; rewards may have a negative effect when they do not incorporate these values.
- Cognition is the mental process of knowing. Cognitive differences are the varied ways people view the world and process information. Instruments such as the Myers-Briggs Type Indicator (MBTI™) and Kirton Adaption/Innovation Inventory (KAI™), are designed to assess cognitive styles. These valuable tools can assist an innovation leader with understanding and leveraging the differences among people.
- Cultural differences are emotionally based. Not understanding and valuing the differences of others

leads to prejudice and other problems. When different characteristics are considered as complementary, they can be leveraged for enormous mutual benefit.

• Sensitivity to gender issues is not only becoming a legal imperative, it also increases the effectiveness of the work place.

Chapter 7—Elements Of Destruction Are Present At Creation

What makes you strong can also destroy you. All innovations have a life cycle: birth, growth, vigor, decline, and death. Constant change enables organizations to recreate themselves, and hence extend their lives. The creation of things includes the creation of hidden features that can be potentially destructive. The innovation leader must be diligent in looking for elements that could imperil the organization.

• Elements of destruction are always present and can be found in:

  ▪ success, when there is an unspoken belief that the product will last forever;
  ▪ personal relationships, when self-interests override common interests;
  ▪ the useful life of a product, or technological limits;
  ▪ the energy of entrepreneurial strength, which can mask the hidden, destructive forces.

• Even when an organization overcomes one destructive element, others are waiting for an opportunity to thrive. Destructive elements are in every organization and are part of every venture. No corrective solution is permanent.

• One of the most potent destructive elements is denial of the existence of destructive forces.

- Defending against forces of destruction includes being aware of their dangers without dwelling on the negative. The best antidote is creating a healthy environment wherein change and innovation can flourish. This can be done, in part, by understanding and utilizing the soft values.

Chapter 8—Soft Values Drive The Organization

Company leaders are under constant pressure to improve the bottom line. This leads to a focus on, if not a preoccupation with, the bottom line, tangible assets, net worth, and P & L statements. However, it is the soft values of the organization's culture that determine productivity. Using an analogy from sports, the soft values are the way the game is played and the bottom line is the scoreboard.

- Among the positive characteristics of soft values are: purity of motive, a positive attitude or spirit, open-mindedness, camaraderie, humility, patience and long suffering, and an attitude of service.
- Among the negative characteristics of soft values are: contentiousness, stubbornness, inordinate pride, discounting or belittling others, passive or uncritical advocacy, indiscriminate criticism, and domineering behavior.
- Soft values are major motivators. Hard values are not.

Chapter 9—Trust Is The Means And Love The Unspoken Word

Trust is essential to sustaining innovation. It reduces friction and enables other parts of the system to work together smoothly, easily, and efficiently. There is no substitute for trust.

- Trust is fundamental to a well-functioning society and is the basis of good working relationships. These relationships include reciprocity, cooperation, and mutual aid.

- Covenantal relationships give stability, energy, and security in a work environment. An explicit covenant should be created because: it is the right thing to do; it provides viability and continuity for the organization; it provides a secure environment wherein fear is reduced; and it is conducive to sustaining innovation.
- In relationship to the organization, I have identified four levels of commitment: partners, stewards, employees, and contractors. Each of these has specific behavioral patterns associated with it.
- There is a spectrum of working relationships among people. Work proceeds best when all concerned share the same perception of that relationship and are prepared to strengthen it.
- "Downsizing" erodes the covenantal relationship, destroys trust, and negatively impacts innovation.
- The commitment qualities of unquestioned loyalty and steadfast devotion are vital when looking for people for positions of responsibility. The competency qualities of a well-trained mind, recognized ability, and mature experience are also essential. Those who can best combine these qualities are the ones who will perform best for an organization.
- Loving the people within the organization is like a glue that maintains a cohesive organization in both good times and bad.

Appendix B

A Glossary Of Innovation Terms

Advocate: A proponent of an idea or proposal.

Black Hole Effect: The unintentional practice of reducing the submission of ideas by non-response.

Bootleg: Work done on projects outside the area of a person's normal billable or chargeable responsibility is referred to as bootleg work. For example, most of the work done through the Office of Innovation is on the originator's own time. This is bootleg time.

Bottom Up: For innovation, "bottom up" means ideas that come from people whose assigned area of work is different from the nature of the idea they are presenting. It has nothing to do with where an originator may be in the organization's hierarchy.

Buy-in: Acceptance of or commitment to an idea.

Challenge Board: A panel designed to examine an idea or solution to make sure that all angles have been addressed.

Champion: A person (sometimes a group) that is devoted to a concept and pursues it relentlessly against all odds; an individual who is willing to become a proponent of ideas at an early stage. This person may have some discretionary money and/or resources available to use in moving an idea forward. Champions take ownership of the idea or a piece of it, and push it. Often there will be a "family" of champions, each one dealing with a specific aspect and/or stage of the process. The originator is the idea's first champion. There are many roles that champions play, including identifying ideas, helping to expand upon them, finding resources necessary to carry ideas to the next step, and identifying other people who can assist in the process until a sponsor is found.

Coaching: This leadership skill is an ongoing process that enables others to develop the ability to solve their own problems and make their own decisions, thereby helping them grow in confidence, self-esteem, commitment, and overall value to the organization. The person, not the problem, is emphasized.

Cognitive Diversity: Differences in how people perceive or act upon their environment; differences in styles people use to acquire and apply knowledge.

Competency: A fundamental characteristic (e.g., motive, trait, self-concept, attitude, value, content knowledge, cognitive, or behavioral skill), causally related to sufficient or superior performance in a job or role; the underlying concept in the theory of competency modeling, developed by David McClelland[71] and others.

Continuous Improvement: Process for incremental improvements that, in their aggregate, lead to cost savings or increased quality.

---

[71]   See D. C. McClelland, "Testing for Competence Rather than Intelligence," in *American Psychologist*, 1973, vol. 28,pp. 1-14.

Council: A small number of people who take on the responsibility for direction and stewardship of an organization. They perform as a "real team" whose members are committed to a common purpose, goals, and working approach for which they hold themselves mutually accountable. They define their work products, and measure what they do as a team against performance goals they set for themselves. (See **Real Team**)

Covenant: A relationship between two or more people within a company, or between the organization and its people, in which each accepts definable (written or oral) responsibility for the mental, emotional, physical, spiritual, and financial well-being of one another; a sacred bond.

Creative Style: The manner in which people interact with their environment when solving problems; a distinction coined by Michael Kirton.[72]

Creativity: Generation of novel ideas or new ways of thinking.

Culture: The attitudes, norms, values, and beliefs that exist in an organization.

Currency of the Realm: The value of an item expressed in the language and behaviors meaningful to those concerned.

Diversity: The differences that occur in any population.

Emotional Intelligence: The ability to be aware of our emotions, manage the negative ones, and harness the positive ones, in order to build passion and energy for individual goals and within teams.

Enhancement: This is a process whereby the innovation advocate works with the originator to refine, develop, and

---

[72]   See Kirton, op. cit.

describe ideas so the ideas will receive serious attention when presented to internal consultants. It is a positive building process, rather than one that discourages. It focuses on what is correct with the concept.

Entrepreneur: An individual who takes on the risk of creating a business to commercialize an idea—their own or someone else's.

Gate: The passage from one stage to another in the development process is like going through a series of doors to get to higher levels of complexity.

Hard Objectives: Tangible objectives (e.g., percent profitability, number of new products launched). (See **Soft Objectives**)

Idea Memorandum: A formal statement that describes the concept and is supported with appropriate drawings, charts and other documents. When complete, it is signed by the originator and witnessed by the innovation advocate.

Ideator: A person who generates many ideas, but has little interest in developing them. Therefore, most of these ideas come to naught.

Innovation: A creative act or solution that results in a quantifiable gain.

Innovation Advocate: A person who assists originators in taking ideas through the agonizing, organizational maze. This includes: helping originators refine and develop ideas in ways that are most apt to get a favorable hearing; locating resources that can be used; coaching and encouraging the originator and subsequent team members as the project goes through its various stages; helping the originator get a perspective of the process; aiding the originator to accept the results, regardless of outcome; and encouraging the submission of more ideas.

Innovation Diversity: The leveraging of diversity within an organization to stimulate innovation.

Innovation Facilitator: See **Innovation Advocate**.

Innovation Leaders: Leaders who support and drive innovation.

Innovation Systems: People-based infrastructures within an organization that facilitate innovation.

Innovator: A person who generates creative ideas and transforms some of them into quantifiable gains.

Internal Consultants: People, generally within an organization, who have expertise in the area of the originator's idea. They review related information and make recommendations for modifications and concept development. They are not directly paid for this service other than their regular salary.

Internal Venturing: A process for launching new businesses that do not fit the company's current lines of business.

Intrapreneur: A term coined by author Gifford Pinchot III that refers to an entrepreneur who stays within a larger organization.[73]

Inventor: A person who discovers a phenomenon or dreams up an idea and then proceeds to transform it into a tangible product. This is usually done on a small scale to meet a need perceived by the person.

---

[73] See Gifford Pinchot, *Intrapreneuring: Why You Don't Have to Leave the Corporation to Become an Entrepreneur,* HarperCollins, New York, 1985.

Office of Innovation: An office created at Eastman Kodak Company to handle new ideas; it was founded in 1979 by Robert Rosenfeld.

Office of Innovation Process: The manner in which ideas are handled by the Office of Innovation. There were five stages to the process at Kodak: idea generation, idea screening, group review, seeking sponsorship, and sponsorship. Other companies have similar processes.

Originator: Someone who comes up with the idea to be developed. The primary responsibility for pushing the idea forward rests with the originator. Sometimes that person has only a vague idea of what is involved, so assistance involves helping the originator know what to expect in trying to gain both acceptance and funding for his or her idea.

Originator-assisted: A process that helps employees transform their ideas into business opportunities. (See Chapter 3)

Paradigm: A set of rules that defines boundaries and describes what to do to be successful within those boundaries.

Paradigm Builder: Someone who solves problems by working within existing structures/paradigms; an alternate term for Kirton's term "adaptor."

Paradigm Pioneer: Someone who solves problems by pushing the limits of existing structures/paradigms or creating new ones; an alternate term for Kirton's term "innovator."

Partner: A person associated with others in some activity of common interest whose identity is entwined with that activity, and who has a deep sense of responsibility with regard to its success or failure.

Physio-cultural: Differences that are readily apparent through observation and interaction (e.g., gender, race, culture, etc.).

Quantifiable Gain: A measurable benefit to the organization.

Real Team: A term by Katzenbach and Smith for a team whose members are committed to a common purpose, goals, and working approach for which they hold themselves mutually accountable.[74]

Relationship Spectrum: A continuum describing the depth of a relationship—on the low end is a loose arrangement or agreement between people, on the high end is a partnership, and, finally, a "covenant."

Sifting: This is a process that separates the ideas with potential from those that have reached the limit of their development. It is associated with gates as well as other circumstances. During the sifting process, the originator, with the help of the innovation advocate, usually realizes when the idea cannot progress any further. When an originator makes the decision to stop pushing the idea forward, it is generally in the light of self-evident information.

Soft Objectives: Objectives related to how people feel as a result of the implementation of a process (e.g., measured in terms of attitudes, job satisfaction, change in corporate climate), as compared to hard objectives which are tangible (e.g., percent profitability, number of new products launched).

Sponsor: People having both the power and ability to allocate funds and/or resources to projects. They can make them

---

[74]   See Jon R. Katzenbach and Douglas K. Smith, *The Wisdom of Teams*, Harper Business Books, New York, 1994.

budgetary line items. When an idea has moved forward to where it has a sponsor, the objective of the Originator-assisted system is completed.

Steward: A person who takes active responsibility for the good of the company as a whole and for its employees; a person who is willing to devote significant time and energy to help others and the company grow, and finds it personally rewarding to do so.

Strategic Transfer: Transfer of technology or knowledge from one point to another for the purpose of leveraging capabilities.

Sustained Innovation: The continuous flow of new products, processes, and services that ensure an organization's competitive edge.

Synergy: An effect that is greater than the sum of its component parts.

Targeted Innovation: Process for developing solutions to meet a specific need.

Trust: Confidence in the integrity, ability, character, and truth of a person or thing.

Type: A classification of personality style based on psychological theory. The Myers-Briggs Type Indicator (MBTI), with 4 dichotomous scales, is a typical indicator tool for personality types.

APPENDIX C

Innovation Systems

Authors on innovation have written about a number of innovation systems. While there are many systems, we have found that they currently fit into one of five categories:

1. *Originator-assisted*
2. *Targeted Innovation*
3. *Internal Venturing*
4. *Continuous Improvement*
5. *Strategic Transfer*

The chart listed in Figure C.1 shows the characteristics of each system.

Figure C.1: Five Systems Chart

Characteristic	Originator Assisted	Strategic Transfer	Targeted Innovation	Internal Venturing	Continuous Improvement
Organization Benefits	A few high-impact business opportunities and cultural change	Reduce development costs and proven technologies	Innovative solutions to specific needs	Very high potential pay-off, expands market base	A large number of incremental improvements leading to cost savings and cultural change
Type of Ideas Solicited	Ideas for new products, technology, or business	Ideas that leverage existing solutions for identifying company needs	Ideas leading to solutions for focused company needs	Ideas for new business that leverage existing core competencies	Ideas leading to increased efficiency or cost savings
Scope of Ideas	Expanding current and developing business interests	Applicable to current needs	Top-down driven; focused on current company needs	Developing new markets	Within current job assignment
Goal of System	Sponsored ideas	Leverage existing technologies	Sponsored ideas	Successful start-up business	Implemented ideas
Time to Reach Goal	6 to 18 months	6 to 18 months	Variable	1 to 5 years	2 weeks to 1 month
Volume of Ideas	Low	Low/Medium	Medium	Low	High
Idea Complexity	High, requiring multi-disciplined evaluation	Can be high, but fitting when needed	Can be high, but with defined disciplines	High, requiring multi-disciplined evaluation	Low to moderate

Characteristic	Originator Assisted	Strategic Transfer	Targeted Innovation	Internal Venturing	Continuous Improvement
Potential Magnitude Per Idea	High	Varies	Medium/High	High	Low
Adoption Rate	From 4-10%	Not Applicable	Variable	1-2%	80% or Greater
Participation Rate	Variable and voluntary	Not applicable (can come from outside source)	High within targeted departments	Low	80% or Greater
Originator Involvement	Originator/innovation advocate drives idea development	"Originator" is content expert during transfer	Originator's idea developed by local management	Varies, generally originator drives new start-up	Originator implements idea within supervisor's authority
Support Mode for Originator	Innovation advocate	Transfer coordinator	Innovation facilitator and local management	Venture coach and portfolio manager	Supervisor
Reward and Recognition	Based on involvement and impact of opportunity (varies)	Traditional company mechanisms (varies)	Traditional company mechanisms (varies)	Based on involvement, risk, impact, and company policies	Small (varies)
Idea Development Process	Opportunity-focused	Needs-focused	Solution-focused	Venture-focused	Idea-focused
Documentation	Comprehensive	Comprehensive	Limited and specific	Comprehensive	Limited/simple
Bias	Expanding and developing business opportunities	Solution-seeding for specific corporate needs	Solving problems	Creating and implementing business plans	Implementation of all ideas

Originator-assisted

An Originator-assisted system is a way of finding unplanned ideas and feeding them into the process of refinement, evaluation, and implementation. This is described in further detail in Chapter 3.

Targeted Innovation[75]

Targeted Innovation system is a way of finding planned ideas to feed this process. Considering that award winning, breakthrough ideas are generally unplanned, you may ask why an organization should opt for a planned approach. Our experience with organizations has demonstrated three major reasons why this might be the system of choice:

1. There may be specific areas where management needs innovative solutions. This calls for a planned or targeted approach, in which people focus their creative energies on the specific problem areas that have been identified.
2. Focusing a system on defined strategic objectives makes it easier to get funding for resources that can be used to help find breakthrough ideas. The organization can fly in top talent or make time and equipment readily available. This approach, when used in conjunction with an Originator-assisted system, can provide the best of both worlds: some concentrated resources focused on an area that management is particularly interested in, plus a system that taps other creative ideas from throughout the organization.
3. The organization or its leaders may desire innovation, but may not be ready for unplanned ideas or they may not view a system for finding unplanned ideas as a priority. While most corporations require, to a certain extent, a

---

[75]   A term originated by Dr. Stanley S. Gryskiewicz, Vice President of Global Initiatives and Senior Fellow, Creativity and Innovation Center for Creative Leadership.

planned approach to efficiently carry out ongoing business processes, some organizations respond to unplanned opportunities more naturally than do others. When leadership has decided to seek such opportunities, a system is needed to fulfill this objective. But the converse is not true: a system will generally not change a leadership or organizational culture by itself. For many organizations, Targeted Innovation is the model that fits their culture most naturally, and with minimal friction with customary procedures.

Indeed, *Targeted Innovation* is the traditional and most common innovation system. Most funded research in organizations is within research and development departments. The guidelines are usually set by top-level executives, who use strategic, long-range planning.

When Ford Motor Company, for instance, decides (targets) what kind of car it wants for a specific market, it pours vast resources into research and development to create a product it hopes will be a big seller like the Taurus. Hopefully, the result is not the disappointment of an Edsel. Putting too many eggs into the wrong basket can be avoided by:

1. Consideration of a diversity of perspectives about strategy, and
2. Frank, objective communication among leaders when reviewing the merits of new and ongoing projects.

Much of the power of Targeted Innovation comes from the fact that the targeting of a specific problem by leaders provides significant motivation to find solutions. This pressure to come up with ideas has led to the use of a wide arsenal of devices for stimulating people's minds to bring out creative ideas. Leaders in creativity, such as Alex Osborn, who gave us brainstorming, and George Prince, who coined the term "synectics," have provided ingenious devices to enhance creativity.

Targeted Innovation, however, is more than just the use of creative techniques. Because teams are generally involved, and because creativity in a team requires a very high degree of functionality, team dynamics are a crucial success factor for Targeted Innovation. Successful "skunk work" operations, such as the Palo Alto Research Center (PARC) at Xerox and the Lockheed Skunk Works, have been extensively studied.[76] Successful innovation teams have demonstrated the importance of the need to invest in and expect the best from people. Generally, in these teams, the members pursue excellence and serve others. They trust each other and relate on a personal level. Often, such teams use a collaborative decision-making model, with a focus provided by the team's clear sense of direction.[77] The importance of a clear statement of purpose is also highlighted in the classic book, *The Wisdom of Teams*[78].

Surprisingly, many corporate creativity sessions begin without a clear, well-thought-out statement of purpose. These efforts often fall short of a breakthrough solution because they focus on obtaining an instant answer to the most obvious question—which, in most cases, is not the critical issue.

Another success factor in Targeted Innovation is the creativity that comes from getting different points of view. We have found that people with different backgrounds add considerably to the Targeted Innovation process, particularly when more breakthrough innovation is desired. We also have found that fresh points of view are necessary for breaking down barriers and preconceptions, and gaining new perspective.

---

[76] Warren Bennis, and Patricia Ward Biedermann, *Organizing Genius*, Addison-Wesley Publishing Company, Inc., Massachusetts, 1997; also, *Audio-Tech Business Book Summaries*, May 1997, vol. 6, no. 5, section 1.

[77] Lawrence M. Miller, *American Spirit: Visions of a New Corporate Culture*, W. Morrow Publishing, New York, 1985.

[78] Jon R. Katzenbach and Douglas K. Smith, *The Wisdom of Teams: Creating the High-Performance Organization*, Harper Business Books, New York, 1994.

Recognizing these success factors, Idea Connections has developed a Targeted Innovation process that consists of three steps: 1) problem/opportunity finding and definition, 2) idea generation, and 3) bringing in outside expertise.

1. The company works with an organization's leadership to attain an accurate definition of the business opportunity, expressed through the development of opportunity statements. These statements are explored and refined until ideas can be generated that point the way toward breakthrough solutions.

2. Cross-functional teams are selected based on criteria established in consultation with leadership. The teams initiate idea generation, or ideation, during which they employ various creativity techniques in the exploration of a topic. The intent of these techniques is to help stimulate breakthrough thinking through experiential, interactive exercises.

3. Following the idea generation phase, the teams develop and articulate the resulting ideas to determine further exploration with a panel of outside experts who provide a fresh perspective. The panel, in conjunction with internal experts, works to generate ideas and articulate the actions needed for implementation.

Another approach to Targeted Innovation is a concept known as a Venture Team. A Venture Team works to develop an idea, and is given a certain amount of autonomy and even part financial ownership of the products it produces. This approach has been used at Signode Industries, Inc., 3M, and Security Pacific.[79]

---

[79]   Phillip D. Olson, "Choices for Innovation-Minded Corporations," *Journal of Business Strategy,* January/February 1990, pp. 42-46; also Robert J. Schaffhauser, "How a Mature Firm Fosters Intrapreneurs," *Planning Review,* March 1986, pp. 6-19.

Internal Venturing

Once an idea comes forward, a decision has to be made about whether that idea fits well enough with the organization's current competencies, strategy, and risk tolerance to proceed with implementation. At this stage, the idea's high potential may be recognized. However, if the idea is for a new product or service, much work remains in terms of researching and developing the market. The potential risk of failure may lead to a decision to abort implementation. If the only ideas that survive the decision-making process are safer, more conservative ones, this may send the message to idea originators that "out-of-the-box" ideas will be disregarded.

One alternative to this sequence of events is the implementation of new and ostensibly independent startup companies using the expertise and core competencies of the parent organization. This is called Internal Venturing. Internal Venturing is entrepreneurship within the organization. Generally, the startup companies seek to prove the given product or service in the marketplace, under their own brand name. This process protects the parent company from some of the consequences of failure if it occurs, and protects the start-ups from the bureaucratic red tape that might exist if one tried to implement the idea through an existing business unit.

Of all the systems, Internal Venturing tends to be the most risky. It usually takes major capital investment, and the probability of success can be discouraging for those desiring easy results. Statistically, out of ten ventures, three will fail quickly. Three will linger and die slowly; three others will continue and make plan. Only one out of the ten will produce a major success, and that may be after a period of several years. This one success can pay for it all! When asked to fund something with only one out of ten chances to have a major success, you can expect a skeptical reception, as each one of the ten can be costly. It is important to define realistic expectations early, and have the buy-in of all major stakeholders.

Internal Venturing also has the most potential for political problems. Innovation is power, like a mythical ring or charm, and the person who holds the ring does so at great risk. When a new venture is started, people who control funding may perceive it as competitive for resources, talent, and customers. They may fear that if the venture is successful, their own operations may be threatened. Funding something like that could be seen as buying their own death warrant. For these reasons, Internal Venturing is used less frequently than other systems, although it has provided some highly successful winners and has the potential to be immensely lucrative.

In talking about success in Internal Venturing, there should be a distinction between financial success and the long-term survival of the system. Here is the paradox: Internal Venturing has had a record of failing in the eyes of the company, but being successful in the eyes of the people who ran it. Companies that maintain substantial Internal Venturing efforts are the exception, though some highly successful ones exist.

As an organization grows, assets also grow, with the result that there's more to risk. People who have a lot to lose are less willing to take risks. Launching a new business takes new thinking. Time needs to be counted differently, based on potentials. The venture needs to be protected from the burden of company overhead. Returns are not immediate and starting markets are not yet large.

Clayton Christensen has pointed out that in order to capture tomorrow's big markets, companies must now capture today's small markets. The difficulty is getting multibillion-dollar companies to undergo the risks involved in what are now only million-dollar markets.[80]

To make *Internal Venturing* work, you need people who have the right skill set for managing the ventures. They need to have good managerial and entrepreneurial skills. They need

---

[80]   Clayton M. Christensen, *The Innovator's Dilemma*, Harvard Business School Press, Boston 1997.

the ability to sell their ideas and influence people in the organization; yet they also must focus on running the business and not playing politics.

Those involved with connecting ventures to the parent company need to understand the dual nature of their role—interfacing with the organization and maintaining the venture's entrepreneurial integrity. If the person responsible for managing the venture's relationship to the parent company thinks only of the venture, or only of the parent company, the venture is likely to get into trouble.

This person, who typically oversees a portfolio of businesses (commonly called a portfolio manager), needs entrepreneurial, managerial, and people skills; he or she has to be able to let the venture managers run their show, and needs to be motivated to help. On the other hand, a portfolio manager must be able to be detached enough to make tough decisions, such as putting an end to a venture that is unlikely to succeed, and putting the people employed by the venture to more productive use.

The parent company also has to evaluate its role in relationship to the venture. Is the parent company functioning in a helpful way, or is it acting more as a hindrance?

Even when a venture is successful, the transition towards making it an official part of the organization can destroy it and the people running the venture may leave.

One company that has apparently found a way out of this potential problem is Thermo-Electron Corporation.[81] Instead of trying to bring successful ventures back into the fold, it lets them remain independent. In essence, the company generates and profits from spin-offs. Other companies, such as IdeaLab, function in a similar way.

Another variant is where corporations set up incubators, charging rent for entrepreneurs to take advantage of their

---

[81]   John R. Wilke, "Innovative Ways: Thermo-Electon Uses," and Clayton M. Christensen, *The Innovator's Dilemma*, Harvard Business School Press, Boston, 1997.

resources. For example, Control Data Corporation set up what it called Business Technology Centers for this purpose. This provides a steady income for the parent company while minimizing the risk and liability involved.[82]

Continuous Improvement

The systems I have discussed so far focus mainly on the beginning and middle parts of the innovation process. What about a product already out to market? The need for innovation continues in the form of incremental improvements. Continuous Improvement is the title generally given to these kinds of systems. Examples include Total Quality Management (TQM) and Kaizen Teian. These approaches produce steady implementations of small, easily enacted enhancements. The success rate is high, and often the large number of innovation successes reported by a company come through this type of system. It has been found that making use of the ideas of those people who are actually doing the hands-on work results in incremental improvements that can save millions of dollars.

This system should not be confused, however, with breakthrough innovation. The major differences are that:

- Incremental improvements have a high success rate, whereas the success rate of break-through innovation is low.
- The benefits of an incremental change are usually seen easily and quickly, whereas the benefits of breakthrough change may not be readily apparent.
- Incremental changes are generally inexpensive, whereas breakthrough change can mean a major financial investment.
- Most importantly, the rewards of incremental innovations are generally modest, but steady, whereas the rewards

---

[82]   James W. Botkin and Jana B. Matthews, *Winning Combinations*, Wiley Publishers, New York, 1992.

of a breakthrough success can be enormous, though less frequent.

As with the other systems, one of the keys to making a Continuous-Improvements system successful is having clear expectations. Some organizations evidence confusion between Originator-assisted systems (targeting more breakthrough ideas) and Continuous Improvement suggestion systems. The expectations are different between these two kinds of systems, and hence the processes and rewards need to be different.

Japanese companies have become famous for their success with Continuous-Improvement systems. The ideas of quality control pioneers W. E. Deming and J. M. Juran were readily accepted by the Japanese during the 1950s and 1960s, long before American companies started taking these ideas seriously. Around the same time, the Japanese were implementing the suggestion system concept that they had seen in their trips to the United States.

A suggestion system is similar to an Originator-assisted system in that it solicits unplanned ideas from employees throughout the organization. It differs from an Originator-assisted system, however, in that once the idea is submitted, the originator is no longer involved. Suggestion systems tend to work well in producing incremental ideas. However, the Japanese variant, part of the Kaizen Teian "little things" philosophy, seems to work even better for producing many small improvements throughout the organization. Often, companies attempt to use suggestion systems to find ideas with big payoffs, but these systems are not designed to enhance ideas to the point where high-potential, high-risk ideas can be properly evaluated. The Originator-assisted model is one way of overcoming that problem.

In Kaizen Teian, however, the emphasis is clearly placed on "little" ideas. Employee participation is emphasized more than the ideas themselves. Successful Kaizen Teian systems frequently achieve a participation rate of 75 to 80 percent, and an adoption rate close to 80 percent as well. Monetary rewards in a Kaizen Teian philosophy are often designed to reward employees' participation in the process and implemented ideas, instead of rewarding the financial impact of the idea. This may be likened to encouraging base hits rather than home runs. If people always try for home runs, they are likely to swing wide and strike out most of the time.

Success factors for Kaizen Teian include the following:

- A high level of participation, which leads to an organizational culture that perpetuates even more participation.
- Effective education of workers on what the organization wants.
- Involvement of employees in the design of the system, to ensure employee buy-in.
- Management commitment.
- Requirement that submissions be related to the employee's job or work area, with approval within the scope of the authority of the employee's manager, thereby preventing the need for a drawn-out approval process. (Ideas that are out of scope may be channeled to another system, such as an Office of Innovation; highly incremental ideas submitted to an Office of Innovation would be referred to the Continuous-Improvement system.)
- Responsibility given to the idea originator to make sure that implementation occurs.
- Local emphasis (although successful ideas may be adopted more globally later).
- Effective supervisor training in the process, which involves understanding how to respond to idea originators, and recognition that it is the originator's responsibility to drive the idea.

The table in Figure C.2 shows how Kaizen Teian achieves large-scale cost savings through small-scale ideas.

Figure C.2: Traditional vs. Teian Suggestion Systems

	Suggestion	Teian
Number of organizations	272	620
Number of eligible employees	8,043,424	2,044,466
Total suggestions received	1,013,421	50,537,412
Number of suggestions per 100 eligible	13	2,472
Number of employees submitting per 100 eligible	8	66.6
Adoption rate	24.0%	80.5%
Average award payments per adoption*	$604.72	$3.53
Average net savings per adoption	$8,075.00	$137.93
Net savings per 100 eligible employees	$24,891.00	$274,475.00

Calculated $1 = 130Yen
*William Golden, Eastman Kodak Company, 1989

Strategic Transfer

Another system is called Strategic Transfer. This system shares new technologies between groups or applies them to new uses. (Sometimes the definition given for the common term Technology Transfer is a little more restrictive, so we have coined the name *Strategic Transfer*.) The transfer may be among departments and divisions within a company; it also works among companies, government agencies, universities, and the private sector. Association meetings and trade shows are places where people learn of new developments and informally start the process of acquiring new technologies. The process is so important that some companies now specialize in helping firms find the technologies they need.

Many companies have had innovation systems that helped them win the innovation battle—only to lose the innovation war. Because as good as a company's ideas are, if people are not open to ideas and opportunities outside their particular organization or area, then at some point they will be left behind.

Many approaches have been taken to make Strategic Transfer happen, including government programs, the monitoring of developments in universities, and databases for linking needs with solutions, to name a few. Unfortunately, our experience is that these approaches have not always given the results that were expected. As I have stressed throughout this book, it is the "people" issues that make or break the innovation process. This is no less true with "strategic transfer" than it is with any other system. Indeed, many of the same issues that an Originator-assisted system deals with have to be tackled to create successful Strategic Transfer. These include the need to overcome the "not-invented-here" syndrome and to demonstrate the value of an idea that's new to a given area or organizational context.

Hence, a successful Strategic-Transfer system has components similar to a successful Originator-assisted system. In particular, someone needs to facilitate the process, once the stakeholders have been identified. Moreover, what holds value for these stakeholders must be understood so that the benefits of change coming as part of the transfer of a technology can be communicated effectively.

Other Systems

One process that is sometimes referred to as an innovation system is *Stage Gate*, which has been written about extensively by Bob Cooper and others.[83] *Stage Gate* systems define the steps involved in idea development and manage the associated risk by using a structured evaluation process (see Appendix B). Some may insist that there are additional innovation

---

[83]   Robert Cooper, "The New Product Process: A Decision Guide for Management," *Journal of Marketing Management*, 1988, 3(3) pp. 238-255.

systems that we did not cover here. In the vast majority of cases, we have found that a system fits fairly closely, or is a hybrid of, one or more of the systems we discussed in this appendix.

Summary

All these various systems are part of the process of innovative systems. Originator-assisted and Targeted Innovation systems feed the process of refinement, evaluation, and implementation, which is generally handled by some variant of a *Stage Gate* process. In the business development phase, Internal Venturing provides an alternate path for an idea (as opposed to implementation through main business units), which allows the company to launch some riskier ideas. Once an idea becomes one of the company's products and services, Continuous Improvement systems help improve that product or service, as well as the processes associated with producing it. This extends the product or service's life in the marketplace. At all stages in the process, Strategic Transfer— a flow of ideas among parts of the organization or from outside of the organization—takes place in the innovative organization, thus preventing it from getting stultified by its own success or by any "not-invented-here" syndromes.

While these are the systems that sustain innovation, it is not necessary for any organization to have all of them in place. Conversely, an organization doesn't have to pick only one. You may find one, two, or several of these as part of an organization's formal infrastructure. In addition, there may be some features of these systems that work informally inside the organization.

After all is said and done, none of these systems will be successful without the application of the Human Principles for sustaining innovation.

Appendix D

Stages Of The Innovation Journey

In Chapter 3, I referred to seven stages an idea goes through to find a sponsor. The last stage covers everything from securing a sponsor to commercial success. These steps make the process seem deceptively simple. In fact, each stage along the way often represents an enormous amount of work and should be considered a major achievement. Some of the steps overlap each other in time, and sometimes the order is different, but these are the stages of the innovation journey. They may be thought of as the hurdles that need to be overcome. With each step there is an evaluation and sifting of ideas, and at each stage a sponsor is needed to provide funding and carry it forward.

(The overall view of this process is the connection of three processes: idea generation, sifting, and securing a sponsor. While a lot of ideas need to come forward, only a few of them can be used. Sifting out unworkable ideas is necessary before searching for a sponsor can begin.)

Figure 3.2 (in Chapter 3) is a diagram of the Originator-assisted system model used at the Eastman Kodak Company.

Following is a bird's eye view outline of the journey of an idea from its creation to the quantifiable gain it generates.

This is not a linear journey. There is a great deal of literature on this subject and readers should refer to the references in the bibliography for further details.

- Concept testing and development. An idea is brought forth and sifted. Those that survive stand in need of a sponsor willing to fund the next step.
- Business analysis. This involves further sifting to see if the idea makes business sense.
- Product development. At this stage, surviving ideas are refined until a product emerges.
- Test marketing. During this stage, it is determined if there is a potential market for the product or service.
- Marketing. Packaging, promotion, and market plans are developed at this time.
- Manufacturing. Now, the product goes into actual production.
- Sales and distribution. This is when the product finally becomes available.
- Customers. The ultimate test of the success of an idea is made by customers, or other final users. They either validate or reject the final form of the idea.

If the idea wins customer approval, represents a substantial saving or profit for the company, or in any other way has significant benefit, the innovation process has completed the journey from idea to quantifiable gain. This is equally true for not-for-profit, profit, and governmental organizations.

APPENDIX E

Innovation Workbook

CHAPTER 1—The Human Component In A Changing World

I.   Think of any project that you have worked on. What hidden principle(s) lay behind it?

II. You have undoubtedly seen a lot of changes in your organization(s). Reflect on the changes you have been involved with.

    A. Was the question of underlying principle ever brought up?

    B. Why or why not?

III. Have you seen successful innovations that did not have the three components of Technical—Business—Human?

    A. If so, what was missing? Why?

    B. If not, why not?

IV.   Based on the characteristics of an innovation leader,

    A. Whom do you know fitting the description?

    B. What motivates them?

    C. How effective are they?

CHAPTER 2—Innovation Starts When People Convert Problems Into Ideas

I.   Look around the room and make a list of everything that is NOT a result of, or been affected by, innovation.

    A. Which of these things did NOT start with an idea?

    B. If you found anything for A. please let me know. Send me an e-mail to the address at the end of Chapter 10.

II.   Some people generate only enough ideas to solve specific problems. Others generate a lot of ideas, whether or not they are related to a specific issue. Still others seldom have new ideas.

    A. If you typically generate no more than the sufficient number of ideas needed to solve a problem:

        1. Find prolific idea generators and ask them:

            a. where they get ideas;

            b. whether or not they prioritize;

            c. to describe a few of their favorite ones;

            d. what kind of reception their ideas get from people with authority within the organization.

        2. How do you think the organization should respond to their ideas? How realistic do you think that is?

        3. Now, find an inventor, and ask him or her the same questions.

4. Next, find an entrepreneur and ask the same questions.

5. If you generate a lot of ideas, talk to someone who does not generate as many ideas, but is methodical and likes clear procedures and established pathways. Ask the person: to describe the way he or she prefers to work how he or she likes it when—in the middle of a project—someone comes forward with a flood of new ideas how he or she responds to the above situation whether he or she prefers to work with change or stability

III.   Who are the best managers in your organization in terms of handling ideas?
       What are their characteristics?

IV.   Why do you think people are afraid of losing their ideas or not getting credit for them?

Chapter 3—Innovation Needs A System

I.   How does an idea move through your organization?

   A. Which of the five innovation systems mentioned in this Chapter, or some variation thereof, are present in your organization?

   B. Which ones need to be either changed or created?

   C. How are ideas funded to become opportunities for development?

   D. If a person has a concept that is a viable business opportunity, but it doesn't fit into the strategic plan of the company, what options are available to make use of that idea?

II.   Talk to an innovator in your organization who has been there a long time. Have the person tell you about a major idea that was important to the company and how it actually developed. If such a person is not readily available, talk to an innovator who has retired. Ask him or her the following:

    A. Who was the real originator of the idea?
    B. To whom was credit given?
    C. How many people were involved in the initial stage?
    D. How was the originator treated?
    E. How did the idea move through the organization?

III. In your organization, how are ideas currently funded to become opportunities for development?

IV. What are the strengths and weaknesses of idea development in your organization's culture?

V. In the past, how have incentives for innovations been handled in your organization?

    A. For incremental innovations?
    B. Revolutionary innovations?
    C. Is the same true today?
    D. In an ideal world, how should they be handled?

VI. Identify two champions in your organization.

    A. What makes them champions?
    B. Why have they been successful?
    C. How would you approach them to support a project?

VII. What system is best suited to your organization's culture? We have selected five components necessary for choosing a system. Each component has alternatives. Using the form in Innovation Figure A, Culture Fit, place a check (3) in the box next to the alternative for each component that best suits your organization. For example find the Organizational Structure component. Ask yourself, "Is your organization Team Based or Hierarchical?" Please choose one.

Innovation Figure A—Culture Fit

COMPONENTS
1. Organizational Structure:
☐ Hierarchy   ☐ Team Based
2. Market Orientation:
☐ Market Pull   ☐ Technology Push
3. Value Discipline:
☐ Product Leadership   ☐ Customer Intimacy   ☐ Operational Excellence
4. MBTI Personality Type:
E = Extraversion   I = Introversion   S = Sensing   N = Intuition
T = Thinking   F = Feeling   J = Judging   P= Perceiving
☐ ENFP   ☐ INTJ   ☐ ESTP   ☐ ENTP   ☐ ESFJ   ☐ ENTJ   ☐ ISTP
5. KAI Creative Style:
☐ Paradigm Builder   ☐ Paradigm Pioneer

VIII. After you have selected the alternatives in Innovation Figure A, Culture Fit, complete Innovation Figure B, Innovation Systems, by placing a check (3) in the box next to the alternatives you selected in Figure A. For example, if you selected Team Based as your alternative for the Organizational Structure component, go to the row in Figure B labeled 1. Organizational Structure and place a check (3) in every column were Team Based appears. Complete this process for all five components. When you have finished, identify which column has the most check marks and look at the Innovation System Category at the top of the column (Originator Assisted, Strategic Transfer, etc.). This system best fits your culture based on the information selected in Figure A. While this system would be the *easiest* to implement, keep in mind that it is not necessarily what your organization *strategically needs* at this time. See Innovation Figure C, Five System Chart, for more information on each of the five system types.

Innovation Figure B—Innovation Systems

INNOVATION SYSTEM CATEGORIES

COMPONENTS	Originator Assisted	Strategic Transfer	Targeted Innovation	Internal Venturing	Continuous Improvement
1. Organizational Structure	□ Team Based	□ Team Based	□ Hierarchy	□ Hierarchy	□ Team Based/ Hierarchy
2. Market Orientation	□ Technology Push	□ Technology Push	□ Technology Push/Market Pull	□ Market Pull	——
3. Value Discipline	□ Product Leadership	□ Customer Intimacy	□ Product Leadership/ Customer Intimacy	□ Product Leadership	□ Operational Excellence
4. Personality Type	□ ENFP	□ ESFJ	□ INTJ/ENTJ	□ ENTP/ENTJ	□ ESTP/ISTP
5. Creative Style	□ Pioneer	□ Builder/ Pioneer	□ Builder/ Pioneer	□ Pioneer	□ Builder

Innovation Figure C—Five System Chart

Characteristic	Originator Assisted	Strategic Transfer	Targeted Innovation	Internal Venturing	Continuous Improvement
Organization Benefits	A few high-impact business opportunities and cultural change	Reduce development costs and proven technologies	Innovative solutions to specific needs	Very high potential pay-off, expands market base	A large number of incremental improvements leading to cost savings and cultural change
Type of Ideas Solicited	Ideas for new products, technology, or business	Ideas that leverage existing solutions for identifying company needs	Ideas leading to solutions for focused company needs	Ideas for new business that leverage existing core competencies	Ideas leading to increased efficiency or cost savings
Scope of Ideas	Expanding current and developing business interests	Applicable to current needs	Top-down driven; focused on current company needs	Developing new markets	Within current job assignment
Goal of System	Sponsored ideas	Leverage existing technologies	Sponsored ideas	Successful start-up business	Implemented ideas
Time to Reach Goal	6 to 18 months	6 to 18 months	Variable	1 to 5 years	2 weeks to 1 month
Volume of Ideas	Low	Low/Medium	Medium	Low	High
Idea Complexity	High, requiring multi-disciplined evaluation	Can be high, but fitting when needed	Can be high, but with defined disciplines	High, requiring multi-disciplined evaluation	Low to moderate

Characteristic	Originator Assisted	Strategic Transfer	Targeted Innovation	Internal Venturing	Continuous Improvement
Potential Magnitude Per Idea	High	Varies	Medium/High	High	Low
Adoption Rate	From 4-10%	Not Applicable	Variable	1-2%	80% or Greater
Participation Rate	Variable and voluntary	Not applicable (can come from outside source)	High within targeted departments	Low	80% or Greater
Originator Involvement	Originator/innovation advocate drives idea development	"Originator" is content expert during transfer	Originator's idea developed by local management	Varies, generally originator drives new start-up	Originator implements idea within supervisor's authority
Support Mode for Originator	Innovation advocate	Transfer coordinator	Innovation facilitator and local management	Venture coach and portfolio manager	Supervisor
Reward and Recognition	Based on involvement and impact of opportunity (varies)	Traditional company mechanisms (varies)	Traditional company mechanisms (varies)	Based on involvement, risk, impact, and company policies	Small (varies)
Idea Development Process	Opportunity-focused	Needs-focused	Solution-focused	Venture-focused	Idea-focused
Documentation	Comprehensive	Comprehensive	Limited and specific	Comprehensive	Limited/simple
Bias	Expanding and developing business opportunities	Solution-seeding for specific corporate needs	Solving problems	Creating and implementing business plans	Implementation of all ideas

IX.   Design a system that could work in your organization to use novel ideas.

    A. What will it look like?

    B. How are you going to make it happen?

    C. Are there any actions you should be taking now?

CHAPTER 4—Passion Is The Fuel And Pain Is The Hidden Ingredient

I.   Does your organization fear or embrace passionate people?

    A. If there is fear, why?

    B. If there are passionate people, are they encouraged or discouraged?

        1. Why?

        2. How?

    C. Do passionate people hold positions of power within your organization?

    D. In what ways could your organization make use of the passion that people have?

    E. What level of passion is acceptable in your organization?

II.   In Chapter 3, Question II, you were asked to interview an innovation leader in your organization. Ask him or her to describe the passion and the pain that went along with a major project.

III.   Do you know anyone who left your organization in the last five years because of the pain caused by their passion?

    A. Was there any potential loss to the organization?

    B. If so, what was it?

   C. Did anyone within the organization seem to be aware of the loss or seem to care?

   D. If so, who?

IV.   **List your direct reports and/or colleagues who have a lot of passion for what they are doing.**

   A. From that list, select the five people who have the most passion.

      1. How do you know they have passion?

      2. Are they successful in what they undertake?

      3. If yes, why?

      4. If no, why not?

      5. What fuels their success?

      6. How are they viewed by:

         a. Their colleagues?

         b. Their managers?

         c. Others within the organization?

         d. People outside the organization?

         e. How many hours a day do they work?

         f. What is their home life like?

      7. Why is the last question important for an innovation leader to know?

   B. Do you belong on this list?

      1. Why?

      2. Why not?

V.   **If you are an executive or manager, answer the following. If not, go on to the next question:**

   A. Who among your direct reports has passion about their work?

1. How important are they to you? Why?
2. How important are they to the organization? Why?
3. What are you doing to sustain their passion?
4. What are you doing that might discourage their passion?
5. What action, if any, do you need to take now?

B. Select the two most important actions that you listed in Question V. above. Write them on a separate piece of paper. Talk about them to someone whose judgment and expertise you respect. If these actions are important to you, create reminders for yourself and place them where you can see them regularly.

VI. If you are not currently in a managerial position, answer the following:

A. Should you be on the manager's list of people with passion?

1. If yes, why?
2. If no, why not?

B. Who inside the organization is helping you to maintain or find your passion?

C. What is there about your organization that encourages passion?

D. What is there about your organization that discourages passion?

E. What can you do to help yourself maintain a high level of passion?

F. What do you need to tell your manager that will help you keep your passion alive?

G. Have you had any ideas that you want to do so much that you would be willing to leave the organization if they won't let you do them?

1. If yes, what are they?
2. If so, why haven't you left?

VII.   Make two columns. At the top of one column write the word "Passion" and then list a few projects that you have gotten excited about. At the top of the other column write the word "Pain" and list the times you have experienced pain while working on a project; be specific rather than general. Then complete the following:

   A.   Look to see where the same project is mentioned in both columns. In those places where there is overlap, ask yourself:

        1.   When you felt the pain, why didn't you quit what you were doing?
        2.   Did the passion ease the pain?

VIII.   From the champions you identified in Chapter 3, Item VIII. who is currently going through some pain because of their passion for what they are doing?

   A.   What kinds of projects excite them?
   B.   What pain has been associated with them?

IX.   Knowing what you know now as an innovation leader, how will you deal with pain and passion in high-risk projects?

Chapter 5—Co-Locate For Effective Exchange

I.   Select three successful projects that have already been completed by a team or a group of people, at least one of whom you know. One of the projects should be a successful new business. The others should be the launch of a successful product, process, or service.

II.   Ask a member of the team (preferably one who was present during the early stages):

     A. How much time did the team members spend together during the first year?

     B. How much time did they spend together after the first year?

     C. When was it most important for them to be together, physically?

     D. What did they get out of their time together?

III.   As things progressed, in all probability they spent less time together.

     A. What effect did that have?

     B. When people were co-locating, why did they get together?

     C. Why did they meet less frequently later on?

IV.   Do you know someone who was in a partnership that dissolved?

     A. What role did co-location play in the building of the partnership?

     B. What role did co-location (or the lack of it) play in the dissolution of the partnership?

V.   Personally speaking, do you prefer to see the person you are dealing with face-to-face when you are making a major business decision or complex purchase, or do you do it by telephone, e-mail, or on the web.

CHAPTER 6—Leverage Differences

I.   Take the Myers-Briggs Type Indicator (MBTI™) and the Kirton Adaption-Innovation Inventory (KAI™), or use some other personality inventory.

     A. Learn what the results of the test mean for yourself.

    B. Give the same tests to the members of your family. Since you already know a lot about them, study the descriptions in relation to their characteristics.

    C. Give the same tests to your colleagues. Study the descriptions in relationship to what you already know about them.

II.   Deliberately get to know people whose types and styles are different from your own.

III.   Think of a project that worked and one that didn't work that included people whose thinking styles differed. How did the different thinking styles contribute to the success or failure?

IV.   Put yourself in the place of others and try to look at issues from the standpoint of different types and styles.

V.   Deliberately get to know people of different physio-cultural groups.

    A. Ask them about their perspectives on a sensitive current issue.

    B. Imagine how you would respond from their perspective.

VI.   List three distinctive functional groups, in addition to your own, that reside within your organization and with whom you have frequent contact. Enter a descriptor in the appropriate box for each group in Innovation Figure D. Then answer the following questions for each group:

    A. What are their unique language characteristics or what special terms do they use?

    B. What are their characteristic problem-solving procedures?

    C. What kinds of things are important to them?

    D. How do they view or define?

Innovation Figure D

CHARACTERISTICS	Group 1	Group 2	Group 3	Your Group
Authority				
Success				
Technology				
Motivation				
Rewards				
What causes stress or frustration				
How sensitive is the group to gender issues				
How sensitive is the group to ethnic issues				

VII. Mentally design a reward system appropriate for each of the above groups.

   A. Compare and contrast the features you thought of
   B. What did you glean from this?

VIII. List three ways in which differences are used constructively and three ways in which they are used destructively in your organization.

IX. What are three things you can do to improve the situation?

CHAPTER 7—Elements Of Destruction Are Present At Creation

I. Reflect on the stories in the chapter and apply the lessons to your own company. What were the seeds of destruction at the origins of your organization?

II.   Are they affecting the company today?

   A. If so, how?
   B. If not, why not?

III.   What seeds of destruction can you see that are
        currently present that, if allowed to continue, could
        have a serious impact on the organization?

   A. What is the most appropriate action that management
      can do about them?
   B. What can you do about them?

IV.   Select the top three products of your company.

   A. What seeds of destruction do they have?
   B. What is their life expectancy?
   C. What can be done to either effectively prolong their useful
      life or replace them?
   D. Who has primary responsibility to make sure the destruction
      of the product does not unduly impact the company?
   E. Given the almost instinctive denial of the need for change,
      what seeds of destruction are you harboring that could
      interfere with your being a more effective innovation leader?
      Among the common ones are: excessive pride in personal
      achievement; inability to share power or the limelight;
      difficulty in accepting and/or acknowledging other people's
      contributions; exaggerated appraisal of one's own personal
      worth or contribution to a project; insecurity; questing for
      power; inappropriate use of power.

V.   When you complete the first draft of your semiannual
        report:

   A. Take 30 minutes to reflect on your greatest success.

B. Either by yourself, or in discussion with someone else who shares your concerns, think carefully about what the seeds of destruction may be that are hidden in the company's successes.

VI. Call in an organizational anthropologist and ask him or her to study your company. From those findings:

A. Look for the things which are conducive to future growth in the company.
B. Look for those factors that can lead to destruction.

Chapter 8—Soft Values Drive The Organization

I. Look at your company's mission and vision statement.

A. List the soft values that contribute to the fulfillment of those statements.
B. To what extent are they visible in the organization?
C. What is the impact of the soft values, for better and for worse?
D. What other soft values are visible in your company's culture, but are not part of the Mission or Vision statements?
E. What are the top three soft values that are important to you as an innovation leader? Why?

II. Think of two effective innovation leaders in your own organization. Ask them what they do to motivate people.

III. Following the directions below, complete the self and organizational assessment tool chart in Innovation Figure E on the next page. The extent to which each of these items is visible will determine whether they contribute to the health and well-being or the deterioration of the organization.

A. Mark the rating you would give your company with a circle (¡).

B. Mark the rating you would give yourself with a square (o).

C. Mark the rating you would give to one of the innovation leaders you named in II with a triangle (r).

Innovation Figure E: Soft Value Characteristics

POSITIVE ELEMENTS	Not Evident				Conspicuous
Purity of Motive	1	2	3	4	5
Spirit	1	2	3	4	5
Open-mindedness	1	2	3	4	5
Camaraderie	1	2	3	4	5
Humility	1	2	3	4	5
Patience	1	2	3	4	5
Service	1	2	3	4	5
NEGATIVE ELEMENTS	Not Evident				Conspicuous
Discord	5	4	3	2	1
Stubbornness	5	4	3	2	1
Pride	5	4	3	2	1
Discounting	5	4	3	2	1
Passive Advocacy	5	4	3	2	1
Indiscriminate Criticism	5	4	3	2	1
Dominance	5	4	3	2	1

Company O	
Yourself □	
Innovation Leader △	

IV.   Add your score

A. 57 or higher: Excellent

B. 43-56: High average

C. 29-42: Low average

D. 28 or lower: Serious need of improvement.

V.   Pick your three lowest scores.

VI.   List specific strategies you plan to use to improve each of them.

VII.   How important do you think these factors are for an innovation leader?

CHAPTER 9—Trust Is The Means And Love The Unspoken Word

I.   What does it mean to have trust?

    A. in your work group?

    B. in the organization at large?

    C. How do you think a greater degree of trust would affect the innovation of your group?

II.   Look at the Commitment Chart (Figures 9.1 and 9.2)

    A. Think of your immediate supervisor or manager. Where does he or she fit on the chart? Put a mark representing her or him on the chart.

    B. Where do you fit on the chart? Put a mark at the appropriate place.

    C. Think of five people who report to you. Where do each of them fit on the chart? Mark the places.

III.   Look at the Comparative Aspects Table (Figure 9.2)

    A. If you have people reporting to you:

        1. Identify one or two key people whom you want to keep inside your organization and are capable of growth in the workplace.

        2. Locate them for the different behaviors listed in the table.

        3. Select two behaviors for each of them. What can you do to help them move to the right on the table?

    B.   If you are an individual to whom no one reports:

        1.   Select five of your peers. Indicate where they belong on the chart.
        2.   Place a mark on the chart for your supervisor.
        3.   Reflect on what you see.
        4.   What actions came to your mind for yourself?

IV.   Look at the Relationship Spectrum (Figure 9.3)

    A. If you have people reporting to you, for the same two people selected above,

        1.   Locate them for the different relationships listed in the spectrum in relation to you.
        2.   Would they put you in the same place?
        3.   What can you do to move the relationship to the right?

    B. If you are an individual to whom no one reports, do the following in respect to yourself:

        1.   Select five of your peers. Place them on the spectrum.
        2.   Place a mark on the spectrum for your supervisor.
        3.   Reflect on what you see.
        4.   What actions came to your mind for yourself?
        5.   Did you think of anything that you can do to benefit the organization?
        6.   What is it and what can you do about it?

    C. List five things that you think are important in making strong covenants with your people.

V.   Identify one act of love within your organization, either from the past or present.

    A. Describe the behaviors—that is, actions that can be seen—that made the above a "loving act."

       B. What do you think motivated the person to act that way?

       C. What can you learn from the above example?

       D. Upon reflecting on this, what, if anything, will you do differently in the future?

VI.   Define what the following working relationships mean in the context of your work group:

       A. Reciprocity

       B. Cooperation

       C. Mutual aid

VII. For a specific task performed in your work group, how would you define the working relationship in the context of the above?

VIII. What can you do to improve the working relationships?

IX.   Pick three people who have the potential to be managers or innovation leaders. Rate them and yourself on a scale of 1 to 5 (1=low and 5=high), according to the following commitment qualities and competencies:

Person	1	2	3	You
Unquestioned loyalty				
Steadfast devotion				
A well trained mind				
Recognized ability				
Mature experience				
TOTAL				

X.   If anyone scores a 1 or 2, do you think you want that person in a leadership position?

BIBLIOGRAPHY

Aaseng, Nathan. *The Inventors. Nobel Prizes in Chemistry, Physics, and Medicine*. Minneapolis: Lerner Publications Co., 1988.

Adain, Gene. *George Washington Carver*. New York: Chelsea House, 1989.

"Bacon, Francis, 1st Baron Verulam and Viscount Saint Albans." *Microsoft® Encarta® 97 Encyclopedia*. CD-ROM. Microsoft, 1997.

Basadur, M. *The Power of Innovation*. London: Pitman, 1995.

"Bell, Alexander Graham." *Microsoft® Encarta® 97 Encyclopedia*. CD-ROM. Microsoft, 1997.

Bennis, W.G., and P.W. Biederman. *Organizing Genius*. Reading, Massachusetts: Addison-Wesley Publishing Company, Inc., 1997.

Botkin, J. W., and Jana B. Matthews. *Winning Combinations: The Coming Wave of Entrepreneurial Partnerships* Between Large and Small Companies. New York: Wiley Publishers, 1992.

Boyd, Thomas A. (ed.). *Prophet of Progress*. New York: E.P. Dutton and Co., 1961.

— Professional Amateur: The Biography of Charles Franklin Kettering. New York: Arno Press, 1972.

Brown, J. S. *Seeing Differently*. Boston: Harvard Business School Press, 1997.

Buchman, D. and S. Groves. *What If? Fifty Discoveries that Changed the World*. New York: Scholastic, Inc., 1988.

Center, Stephen. B. "The Diversity Journey." *Human Resource Professional*, Issue 307, July 12, 1996.

Christensen, C. M. *The Innovator's Dilemma*. Boston: Harvard Business School Press, 1997.

Cooper, Robert. "The New Product Processes: A Decision Guide for Management." *Journal of Marketing Management*, 1988.

"Corporate Downsizing, Job Elimination and Job Creation." *1996 AMA Survey*, Summary of Key Findings.

DeMarco, D. and J. Felberg. "New Idea Enhancement at Amoco Chemical." *Journal of Product Innovation Management*, 1992.

— "The Role of the Innovation Facilitator." *Chemtech*, 1992.

Doughty, D. and E. H. Bowman. "The Effects of Organizational Downsizing on Product Innovation." *California Management Review*, 1995.

Drucker, P. *Innovation and Entrepreneurship*. New York: Perennial Library, 1985.

Evolanoff, Michael and Marjorie Beckman. *Alfred Nobel, the Loneliest Millionaire*. Los Angeles: W. Ritchie Press, 1969.

Fink, Donald G. "Facsimile." *Collier's Encyclopedia*. New York: Collier's, 1996.

Freedman, G. *The Pursuit of Innovation: Managing the People and the Process that Turns New Ideas into Profit*. New York: American Management Association, 1988.

Frederick, Jim. "The End of Eureka!" *Working Woman*. February 1997.

Friedel, Robert. *Zipper: An Exploration in Novelty*. New York: Norton, 1994.

Fukuyama, F. Trust: *The Social Virtues and the Creation of Prosperity*. New York: Free Press Paperbacks, Simon and Schuster, 1995.

Gladwell, Malcolm. *The Tipping Point: How Little Things Can Make a Big Difference*. Boston: Little Brown, 2002.

Gordon, W. J. *Synetics: The Development of Creative Capacity*. New York: Harper and Row, 1961.

Gryskiewicz, Stanley S. *Positive Turbulence: Developing Climates for Creativity*, Innovation, and Renewal. California: Jossey-Bass Publishers and the Center for Creative Leadership, 1999.

Gryskiewicz, S. S., and D. A. Hills. *Readings in Innovation*. Greensboro: Center for Creative Leadership, 1992.

Hast, Adele (ed). *Company Histories: Vol. V*. Chicago: St. James Press, 1991.

Haustein, H.D., and H. Maier. Innovation and Efficiency: Strategies for a Turbulent World. New York: Pergamon Press, 1985.

Higgins, J. M. *Innovate or Evaporate: Test and Improve Your Organization's I.Q.—Its Innovation Quotient*. Winter Park, Florida: New Management Publishing Company, 1995.

"History of the Helicopter." *Microsoft® Encarta® Reference Library*. CD-ROM. Microsoft, 2002.

Imparato, N., and O. Harari. *Jumping the Curve: Innovation and Strategic Choice in an Age of Transition*. San Francisco: Jossey-Bass Publishers, 1994.

"International Code of Signals." *Microsoft® Encarta® 97 Encyclopedia*. CD-ROM. Microsoft, 1997.

Jane, H., and D. Walker. *Managing Innovation*. London: Sage Publications, 1991.

Kanter, Rosebeth Moss. *When Giants Learn To Dance*. New York: Simon and Schuster, 1989.

Katzenbach, J.R., and D.K. Smith. *The Wisdom of Teams: Creating the High-Performance Organization*. New York: Harper Business Books, 1994.

King, Martin Luther, Jr. Public domain sermon, delivered at Dexter Avenue Baptist Church. Montgomery, Alabama: November 17, 1957.

Kirton, M. J. "Adaptors and Innovators: A Description and Measure." *Journal of Applied Psychology*. Vol. 61, 1976.

—. *Adaptors and Innovators: Styles of Creativity and Problem Solving*. 2d ed. London: Routledge, 1994.

"Kitty Hawk." *Microsoft® Encarta® Reference Library*. CD-ROM. Microsoft, 2002.

Koestler, Arthur. *The Act of Creation*. New York: Macmillan, 1964.

Kolstoe, John. *Developing Genius*. Oxford: George Ronald, 1995.

Krebs-Hirsh, Sandra and Jean M. Kurnmerow. *Introduction to Type in Organizations*. 2d. ed. California: CPP, 1987.

Kuczmarski, T.D. *Innovation: Leadership Strategies for the Competitive Edge.* Lincolnwood, Illinois: NTC Business Books, 1996.

Leonard-Barton, D. *Wellsprings of Knowledge: Building and Sustaining the Source of Innovation.* Boston: Harvard Business School Press, 1995.

Levering, Robert and Milton Moskowitz. *The 100 Best Companies to Work for in America.* New York: Currency/Doubleday, 1993.

"Lucien." *Microsoft® Encarta® 97 Encyclopedia.* CD-ROM. Microsoft, 1997.

"Malden Mills: What a Great Place to Work." *National Association of Working People.* Vol. 1, No. 1, August 1996.

Marcic, D. *Managing with the Wisdom of Love: Uncovering Virtue in People and Organizations.* San Francisco: Jossey-Bass Publishers, 1997.

McClelland, D. C. "Testing for Competence Rather than Intelligence." *American Psychologist.* Vol. 28, 1973.

McCraty, Rollin, Mike Atkinson, Dana Tomasino and William Tiller. "The Electricity of Touch: Detection and Measurement of Cardiac Energy Exchange Between People." *Proceedings of the Fifth Appalachian Conference on Neurobehavioral Dynamics: Brain and Values.* Mahwah, New Jersey: Lawrence Erlbaum Associates, Inc., 1997.

Miller, L. M. *American Spirit: Visions of a New Corporate Culture.* New York: W. Morrow Publishing, 1985.

Miller, W. *Quantum Quality: Quality Improvement Through Innovation Learning and Creativity.* White Plains, New York: Quality Resources, 1993.

Moore, Tom. "Building Credibility in a Time of Change." *Communication World Online,* 1996.

Olson, Phillip D. "Choice for Innovation-Minded Corporations." *Journal of Business Strategy,* January/February 1990.

Osborn, A.F. *Applied Imagination.* New York: Charles Scribner's Sons, 1963.

Page, Albert L. "Presentation to Product Development & Management Association." Chicago, November 13, 1991.

Panati, Charles. *Panati's Extraordinary Origins of Everyday Things*. New York: Harper & Row, 1987.

Peak, Martha. "Cutting Jobs? Watch Your Disability Expenses Grow." *Management Review*, March 1997.

Pinchot, Gifford, III. *Intrapreneuring: Why You Don't Have to Leave the Corporation to Become an Entrepreneur*. New York: HarperCollins, 1985.

Poe, Edgar Allan. *The Weekly Mirror*. New York, 1845.

Robinson, A. G., and S. Stern, S. *Corporate Creativity: How Innovation & Improvements Actually Happen*. San Francisco: Jossey-Bass Publishers and Berrett-Koehler Publishers, 1997.

Rosenfeld, R. "Innovation Through Investment in People: The Consideration of Creative Styles." Excerpt from *Key Issues in Creativity Innovation & Entrepreneurship*, 1991.

Rosenfeld, R. and J. Servo. "Business and Creativity: Making Ideas Connect." *The Futurist*, 1984.

— "Facilitating Innovation in Large Organizations." *Innovation and Creativity at Work*, 1990.

— "The First Step to Implementing New and Better Ideas." *Intrapreneurial Excellence*, 1985.

Rosenfeld, R., M. Winger-Bearskin, D. Marcic and C. Braun. "Delineating Entrepreneurial Styles: Application of Adaptation-Innovation Subscales." *Psychological Reports*, 1982.

Rosenfeld, R., M. Winger-Bearskin, D. DeMarco and C. Braun. "Entrepreneurs: Who Are They and How Do We Find Them? A KAI Study." Research paper, 1992.

Samuelson, R. J. "The Assembly Line." *Newsweek Extra*. Winter 1997-1998.

Sanderson, S.W., and M. Uzumeri. *The Innovation Imperative: Strategies for Managing Product Models and Families*. Chicago: Irwin, 1997.

Savidge, J. *The Pathmaster Guidebook*. Helsinki: The Finish Academies of Technology, 1993.

Schaffhauser, Robert J. "How a Mature Firm Fosters Intrapreneurs." *Planning Review*. March 1986.

Smith, G.P. *The New Leader: Bringing Creativity and Innovation to the Workplace*. Delray Beach, Florida: St. Lucie Press, 1997.

Stern, K. and M. K. McClintock. "Regulation of Ovulation by Human Pheromones." *Nature*, Vol. 392, 1998.

Stern, Sam. *The Relationship Between Resource Development and Corporate Creativity in Japan*. Human Resource Development Quarterly, 1992.

Taylor, Frederick Winslow. *The Principles of Scientific Management*. New York: Harper Brothers, 1911.

Townsend, Robert. *Up the Organization*. New York: Alfred A. Knopf, Inc., 1970.

Tushman, M. L., and C. O'Reilly, III. *Winning Through Innovation: A Practical Guide to leading Organizational Change and Renewal*. Boston: Harvard Business School Press, 1997.

Utterback, J.M. *Mastering the Dynamics of Innovation*. Boston: Harvard Business School Press, 1994.

Von Braun and Ordway. "Apollo Program." *Encyclopedia Americana*. Grolier Incorporated. Vol. 25, 2000.

Wallas, Graham. *The Art of Thought*. New York: Harcourt, 1926.

West, M., and J. Farr. *Innovation and Creativity at Work: Psychological and Organizational Strategies*. West Sussex: Wiley Publishers, 1990.

Whiting, B., and G. Solomon. *Creativity, Innovation and Entrepreneurship*. Buffalo, New York: Bearly Limited, 1989.

Wilke, John R. "Innovative Ways: Thermo-Electron Uses." *In The Innovator's Dilemma*. Boston: Harvard Business School Press, 1997.

Yenne, Bill and Dr. Morton Grosser (ed). *100 Inventions that Shaped World History*. California: Bluewood Books, 1993.

Zangwill, W. I. *Lightening Strategies for Innovation: How the World's Best Firms Create New Products*. New York: Lexington Books, 1993.

AUTHOR'S BIO

R obert Rosenfeld began his 19-year career at Eastman Kodak Company as a chemist, but soon grew interested in the human side of the innovation process and founded Kodak's Office of Innovation, which helped transform ideas into hundreds of millions of dollars in revenues. In 1988, Bob founded Idea Connections, a consulting firm which has brought him into numerous large companies worldwide and has established his reputation as a leader in the field of innovation. Throughout his career, Bob has been dedicated to creating environments that foster the creative spirit.

Bob and his wife Debbie have seven children and live in Rochester, New York.

INDEX TERMS

A

Advocate 57
American Management
    Association 157
Amstutz, Noah 24
Anderson, Richard 147
Apple Computer 159
Archimedes 90
Armstrong, Neil 38, 86
Avery, Sewell 138
Avis Rent A Car System, Inc.
    165

B

Bacon, Bob 83
Bacon, Sir Francis 26
Bain, Alexander 24
Bakewell, Frederick 24
Belin, Edouard 24
Bell, Alexander Graham 38
Bell Telephone Company 39
Black Hole Effect 195
Bootleg 195

Bottom Up 195
Bowman, Edward H. 157
Braun, Don 163
Business Concept and
    Documentation 57
Buy-in 195

C

Camaraderie 146
Carey, G. R. 24
Carothers, William 47
Carver, George Washington 87
Caselli, Giovanni 24
Celento, Frank 60
Celento, Loretta 60
Center, Stephen B. 124
Challenge Board 195
Champion(s) 58, 196
Chaparral Steel 144
Co-location 102, 104
    effectiveness of, Figure of
        106
    managing 107

Printed in the United States
72460LV00003B/118-324